Duty and the Law

Judge John J. Parker and the Constitution

Judge John J. Parker

Duty
and
The Law

Judge John J. Parker
and the
Constitution

By

William C. Burris

Professor of Political Science
Guilford College

COLONIAL PRESS

Also by William Burris:

Analyzing American Politics: A New Perspective
(with Walter Roenbaum & John Spanier)

Publisher's Special Acknowledgment

Special gratitude to Pat Atkinson of Bayou Graphics,
Covington, Louisiana, for typography, and design.

Contents

Preface

Judge John J. Parker of Charlotte, North Carolina, was, at the time of his death in 1958, the Senior Judge of the United States Courts of Appeal. He was well known and highly respected by the lawyers and judges who worked with him during his long tenure on the federal bench. But he is not well known to American historians, even those who specialize in constitutional history or the history of the federal courts. If he is remembered, it is as the only nominee to the United States Supreme Court to be rejected by the United States Senate in the first half of this century.

But John J. Parker was not just another federal judge who happened to gain a footnote in history because of a single vote in the Senate. According to Judge Harold R. Medina, Parker was one of two men in this century who stood above all others in their qualifications to become Supreme Court Justices but were never advanced to the nation's highest judicial tribunal. The other man, Judge Learned Hand of the Second Circuit Court of Appeals, was never even honored with a nomination. Both men remained on their respective appellate courts throughout their careers and made important and lasting contributions to American Constitutional Law and American public life. But neither has received the degree of public attention given to the Justices of the Supreme Court, however ordinary their records and contributions.

Judge Hand has fared better in this respect than Judge Parker. Hand lived and worked in New York, closer to the center of American scholarly and intellectual life. He was an extraordinarily gifted writer whose articles and opinions sparkled with graceful phrases and similes and thus was a more interesting and attractive figure to those who write about American judges. Judge Parker lived and worked in the provinces, somewhat removed from the American mainstream. He was born and educated in the American South and served his entire judicial career on the Fourth Circuit Court of Appeals in Richmond, Virginia. Moreover, Parker was more the man of action; he came to the federal bench not from the cloistered towers of the Eastern Establishment but as a young lawyer-politician from the rural South. He was well-marked by the partisan conflicts of his era and bore the social, intellectual and racial stigmata of his home region.

Throughout his career, Judge Parker had one overriding concern: the preservation of American democracy through the application of the great general clauses of the American Constitution to a changing society. These great clauses could only be preserved through reinterpretation by judges working within a fair and efficient judicial process that enjoyed the trust and support of the people. Liberty and restraint were the two essential elements in democracy, and the function of law was to preserve both in the body politic. It was the duty of judges to accomplish this task — molding and modernizing the great principles of the Constitution to make them relevant and applicable to changing modes of life and thought.

The theme of these essays is that Judge Parker must be seen as a man of his times. Shaped by the culture of the post-Civil War South, he became an appellate court judge who, bound by duty to keep the law straight according to the precedents of the Supreme Court, was called upon to square the Constitution with new expectations and demands in a restless and changing society. As a judge he attempted to affirm principle over expediency, law over privilege, precedent over passion, justice over legal technicalities, and gradual reform over revolutionary change. His commitment to law, to the tenuous but fundamental balance between liberty and restraint placed him athwart the path of many groups and forces that demanded rapid and immediate change in the circumstances of their lives, as well as the entrenched combinations of political and economic power that resisted all change. In all cases, Judge Parker attempted to do his duty—his duty to God, the Constitution, and his own conscience. And he suffered the consequences.

This study deals with the major political and constitutional events in Judge Parker's public career. It attempts to draw from these events his views on the problems and promise of the American experiment in democratic government. It is written for the general reader; therefore, it does not use the form of documentation normally found in legal or scholarly studies. The sources of quotations are readily identifiable in the text, and the principal sources upon which this study is based are listed in the appendix.

No summary of John Parker's life could do him justice if it failed to note the way his faith in God and his steadfastness in the path of duty enabled him to carry on and so grow in stature and accomplishment as to approach the very ideal of what a man of law can be.

Judge Harold R. Medina

I

Place and Time

He was a lawyer even as a boy.

S. I. Parker

The place and time of a man's birth and formative years are two important facts about his life. This is merely another way of saying that culture is an important force in shaping human thought and behavior. Early habits and values, modes of thought, cultural norms and affections remain persistent forces in the human mind. We never fully break away from the conditions and circumstances that set us on our way. The prevailing values of the home place, the influences of family and neighbors and the historical conditions of the era in which we grow up remain a part of us; they continue to shape our view of ourselves and our view of the world.

A Southern Town

John J. Parker was a Southerner. He was born, reared, educated and lived his entire life in the Piedmont section of North Carolina. And, despite his rise to national prominence as a jurist, he remained a Southerner in his affections and loyalties. His Southern roots were deep and the Southern past belonged to him; its poverty, pride, promise and cultural values were all a part of his makeup. And, because of his prominence as a politician and federal judge and his involvement in the nation's most controversial public issues over a fifty year period, he became a part of its history.

He was born John Johnston Parker in Monroe, North Carolina on November 20, 1885, the eldest son of John Daniel Parker and Frances Johnston Parker. At that time Monroe was a small market town with only a few thousand inhabitants. It was the county seat of Union County, a rural section of the state lying along the South Carolina state line just south of Charlotte. The people of Monroe were poor, hard-working, proud, self-reliant, religious and hard pressed by the social and economic deprivations of the Civil War and Reconstruction. Yet, they were generally optimistic about the future. The white people of the area were of English and Scotch-Irish ancestry, and almost all were engaged in farming or small trades. There were few, if any, wealthy families; hard work, doing without, getting by and making do were their daily concerns. The black people of the area were locked in at the bottom of the economic scale. They were much worse off than the whites; they did not have the hope for the future, the promise of better times or the opportunities to improve themselves. Blacks were expected to "stay in their place" and they did so. Race relations were personal and, at least on the surface, kindly rather than distant and hostile. Racial segregation was a legal and cultural fact of life, fully understood by both races.

Social class, as the term is used and understood today, is not very useful when applied to little towns like Monroe during these years before the turn of the century. Some families were better off than others: successful tradesmen, public employees, cotton brokers, lawyers, ministers and physicians. They lived in bigger houses, enjoyed higher living standards and filled the positions of leadership in the community. But the great majority of families were composed of working people who lived on their daily wages. Their horizons and their hopes for the future of their children did not extend beyond the boundries of the local community. Children were expected to get a little schooling, get a job and take care of themselves. Expectations were not high that the children would rise beyond the level of their parents.

But some working class families were different. Despite close similarities in income, occupation and social standing there was a special element at play in these families that set their children apart from the majority. It was an element of hope, optimism and a sense of progress; an impulse that encouraged their children to move up and out into the wider world, to make something of themselves, to achieve positions of leadership and make a contribution to mankind. This distinction was a kind of "spark" that gave a special quality to children. These families were not rich or prominent; they could not finance an education at the state university or private colleges; and they could not provide entree to the professions or assist their children in making the kind of social contacts that would open doors in the business world. Although this distinction is difficult to define, it was very real; and it is of major importance in understanding the sources of Southern leadership during this era. These families, set apart because of the values instilled in their children, produced many of the religious, educational and political leaders of the South during the period between the Civil War and the beginning of World War II. John J. Parker grew up in this kind of family.

Parker's father Daniel, or "Dan" as he was known in Monroe, had very little formal education. He was an ordinary working man, earning a living for his family in a variety of jobs: a cotton gin, foundry and eventually as the owner of a small meat market. He was a Baptist, and a descendant of a large Union County family, the kind of family with many branches that maintained contact with each other and often held reunions. He was descended from Peter Parker, a soldier in the Revolutionary War and Leonidas Parker, a Confederate soldier who died in the Battle of Chancellorsville during the Civil War. Few members of the Parker family obtained positions of influence beyond their local communities until John J. Parker rose to prominence in state politics and the federal judiciary. But, as they say in Union County, the Parker family "was of good stock, folks you can depend on."

But Parker's ancestry on his mother's side is another story. She was Frances Johnston of Edenton, North Carolina, the daughter of Rev. Samuel Iredell Johnston, a prominent Episcopal clergyman and Mary Burgwyn Johnston. Through his mother's family Parker was directly related to Samuel Iredell Johnston, a Surveyor-General of the colony of Carolina who came to America from Scotland in 1735, Abner Nash, Governor of North Carolina in 1780, Samuel Johnston, Governor of North Carolina in 1787, and James Iredell, one of George Washington's early appointments to the United States Supreme Court.

Parker's mother is remembered in Monroe with much respect and admiration. She was a music teacher, trained at St. Mary's College in Raleigh, who came to Monroe with a sister who was employed as a telegraph operator by the railroad. She was one of the founding members of the small Episcopal church in the town and the three children were raised in this faith. She was a refined and gracious lady and citizens of Monroe who were contemporaries of Parker say that the children were molded in her image. One elderly gentleman who knew the Parker family well said of Judge Parker; "The finest blood in North Carolina flowed in his veins. And every fine quality, except one, he received from his mother. He got his boundless energy from his father." Parker loved and admired his father and was unusually attentive and solicitous toward him all his life. But there is little doubt that Parker's spiritual and educational inspiration came from his mother.

Parker went to work in his father's meat market at the age of thirteen. He later worked as a stock-boy and clerk at Belk's store, at the county fair in the summer months and at other odd jobs around Monroe. It is said of him that even as a boy "he never learned to play." He was a serious-minded youth; he did not play ball and romp in the fields surrounding the town as the other boys did. Indeed, he was often teased by the local boys and taunted with the name, "Johnny Bull." Whether he was tagged with this name because of his work in the market or because of his habit of talking too much is not known. Most likely, the latter reason is the correct one because Parker is remembered as an unusually opinionated youth who was interested in everything and had something to say on every topic. Parker is also remembered as being an unusually bright and intelligent youth who took an early interest in politics and public affairs. His brother, Samuel Iredell Parker,* remembers this side of his character very vividly, remarking that John "was a lawyer even as a boy." Parker excelled in school, especially in Greek, and took delight in debating contests that allowed him to test himself against others. Before he finished high school he had decided to become a

---

*A highly decorated Army officer during World War I.

lawyer, and made plans to enter the University of North Carolina to prepare himself for this profession. But, the family had no money to finance his education. If he was to earn a university degree, he would have to do it on his own.

The University

The University of North Carolina at Chapel Hill proved to be the making of John J. Parker as a man, lawyer, politician and federal judge. He remained intensely loyal and supportive of the school all his life, supporting it financially, serving on its Board of Trustees, and defending its faculty and presidents during difficult times. As a mature man, Parker had no personal hobbies or diversions from his work. His son, Francis I. Parker,* has said that the only hobby his father had was the University of North Carolina. Like so many of its graduates, especially those who studied there when it was a small, intimate institution, Judge Parker never really left the University.

Parker arrived in Chapel Hill in 1903, as a big, strapping, opinionated eighteen year-old country boy standing well over six feet tall with a large head and high brow. And, if we are to believe the comments of his fellow students, he arrived with a superior attitude, a certain lack of patience with the foibles of others, and something of a fixation about being in charge of everything around him. He had a good reading knowledge of Greek, a keen interest in history and logic and a determination to excell and to test himself against both students and faculty. Chapel Hill at the turn of the century was a different world from what it is today. It was a small, rural, isolated village. The University

---

*Associate Justice of the North Carolina Supreme Court.

was small, distinctly Southern in its makeup and tone and committed to a classical mode of education. There were few diversions, except those created by the students themselves. If Parker ever frolicked about and wasted his time, there is no record or memory of either. Little or no money came from home and he supported himself and paid his bills by selling suits for a Baltimore clothing firm. He took measurements, placed orders and delivered the suits to his fellow students. In later years he was amused when reminded by some former students that they had purchased their "first whole suit with long pants... for $12.50" from a man who was about to become a Justice of the Supreme Court.

Parker's undergraduate program consisted of courses in English, math, physics, chemistry, Latin, Greek, French, philosophy, economics and history. He completed his undergraduate studies in three years, earning the highest academic average in the history of the University up until that time. His only "C" grade was in a logic course under Professor Horace Williams. "Old Horace," as Williams was always known, had this to say about Parker: "We fought like tigers from the first day of the course as John would accept no thought unless it was made a part of his own thinking." Explaining the "C", Williams said, "my A's are saved for that person who is interested in philosophy as a professional matter, which John was not." Among his fellow students, Parker was known as one of "Horace's Cranks" because of the amount of time he spent both in and out of class, jousting with his eccentric mentor. After graduation, Parker became an active member of that fraternity of Chapel Hill graduates known as "Old Horace's Boys," a group of men who enjoyed a special relationship with this most colorful figure in the folklore of the

University. The two maintained an active correspondence over a thirty year period after Parker left the University. Williams made it a practice to read Judge Parker's opinions and often wrote to congratulate him on his logic and reasoning. Commenting once on a case in which Parker had reversed a district court judge, Williams said that if he were the district judge he would "crawl in a hole" after reading Parker's analysis of the law. In another letter Professor Williams told his "C" student that the logic and analysis of his judicial opinions reminded him of Chief Justice Marshall.

Parker was involved in campus politics throughout his career at Chapel Hill. He was elected president of his class during his freshman year and again in his senior year. He was president of the Student Council and was tapped for membership in the Order of the Golden Fleece. Parker refused to accept this honor and would not agree to be inducted into this organization.* He saw it as an elitist group, undemocratic both in its selection procedures and in the principles upon which it was founded. This rejection was consistent with his general attitude toward other features of campus life that he believed to be undemocratic. He was an outspoken opponent of the practice of hazing freshmen, which he regarded as stupid, silly and dangerous, and he opposed the fraternity system because he believed it perpetuated distinctions among the students that were unfair.

These incidents, actions, and attitudes are of little importance when taken separately. But, when taken together, they tell us something about Parker as a young student that helps explain his latter behavior as a politician and judge. As a student he was an "independent spirit" who would not move with the crowd. He would say what he

---

*Parker accepted membership in the Golden Fleece several years after leaving the University.

believed even though everybody around him disagreed. He was suspicious of rank and high position when it rested on privilege that had not been earned. Rewards should come to an individual because of what he accomplished, not because of who he was or the groups or circles to which he belonged. Parker wanted honors; he wanted to excell and to lead, but he wanted only positions or honors that he had earned. And he usually succeeded in winning the prizes he hoped to win: the presidency of the campus chapter of Phi Beta Kappa, the Alexander Prize in Greek, the Magnum Orator's Medal and the University's highest honor for leadership in student government.

In 1906, Parker entered the law department of the University, the goal he had set for himself in high school. He continued to support himself by selling suits and teaching the introductory course in Greek in the undergraduate college. The law department was very small; approximately eighty students were in residence and only three professors were engaged in full-time teaching. James Cameron MacRae was dean and professor of common law and statute law; Lucius Polk McGehee was professor of law and equity; and Kemp Plummer Battle was professor of constitutional history and international law. Charles Lee Raper gave lectures in economics, and Charles S. Manson in medical jurisprudence. Members of the local bar gave special lectures on other areas of the law. The first year of study consisted of courses in the law of persons, property, torts, contracts and criminal law. The second year involved lectures in equity, procedure, evidence, public and private corporations, constitutional and international law, administration, insurance, bankruptcy and admiralty law. Traditional teaching methods were used: testbooks, lectures, the reading of selected cases and moot court. Sessions of moot court were held weekly, concentrating on both criminal and civil cases. The students were involved in the preparation of cases for trial, drawing of pleadings, selection of jurors, examination of witnesses, arguments of law and fact to judge and jury and the preparation of appeals.

The students of course were being trained to practice law. But, the fundamental objectives of the law program were scholarly and academic in nature. Students were taught to understand the great principles of the law and "to show that legal principles lie imbedded in basic conceptions of justice and right." The point was to learn the underlying reasons "for propositions of law rather than the concrete propositions themselves." The ultimate purpose was to encourage students to understand the theoretical principles of law and to develop their "reasoning faculties in the logical application of these principles to practical statements of fact."

Parker took these rather elevated ideas about the objectives of legal education completely to heart. His philosophy of the law, as revealed in later years in opinions, articles, speeches and private correspondence, deviates hardly at all from the basic premises of his legal education at Chapel Hill. He believed firmly, and declared publicly over a period of thirty-three years on the federal bench, that the law was more than a collection of rules made by man. Law was a series of eternal principles of justice and right that arose out of the natural order of life. Lawyers and judges, more than any other profession, were responsible for the interpretation of these enduring principles in the light of changing historical conditions. The ultimate objective to be served was not the law itself, but the freedom and dignity of the individual. In 1923, when the University was making plans to adopt the case method of instruction in order to keep pace with the direction of legal education in the rest of the country, Parker then a prominent attorney in Charlotte, objected strongly to H. W. Chase, President of the University. In essence, he said that the only reason this change was being made was because the University felt some sort of compulsion to follow the lead of Harvard University. After a prolonged and detailed defense of the lecture method of instruction and the required reading of such classics as *Blackstone's Commentaries*, Parker appealed for the preservation of a program in legal education that taught students the great and abiding principles of law. He concluded his letter to President Chase with a sense of regret and a touch of sarcasm: "If the function of a law school is to produce law clerks, then the case system is the system to follow."

Parker maintained the same kind of academic record in law school that he had achieved in the undergraduate college. In his final year he was awarded the Bryan Prize for the best thesis on a legal subject. It was said of him, as his university days drew toward an end, that no position in North Carolina was beyond his reach if he chose to pursue it. The road to Chapel Hill had been the road up and out of a small rural town. The University had been both a testing ground and an inspiration. He had entered its freshman class as a talented, ambitious, independent and out-spoken young man with no advantages stemming from wealth, social standing or family connections. He left the University in 1908 at the age of twenty-three knowing full well that he had to make it on his own; but he was more confident than ever of his abilities, and in his determination to achieve a position in life that would allow him to exercise leadership. His university experience had strengthened his resolve to become a lawyer and to look forward to a career in public affairs.

If Parker had chosen to attend Wake Forest, Trinity, Guilford or Davidson he might possibly have become a Christian minister. He had grown up in a strick religious home and he had been active as a boy in his church. He believed in the principles of the Christian faith and, as an undergraduate, attempted to live his life according to a set of moral understandings that he believed should shape the lives of all men. These beliefs and his commitment to them did not change when he became a prominent politician and federal judge. In articles and speeches, he said, again and again, that American democracy was the political expression of the basic religious principles embodied in the Christian tradition.

The climate of a Christian college and the large number of able students in these insitutions studying for the ministry might well have drawn Parker in that direction. Had this happened, the church would have been the better, but the world of public affairs would have lost a distinguished public servant. But, Parker's boyhood interest in becoming a lawyer had led him to Chapel Hill and this decision proved to be one of the most crucial choices of his life. At Chapel Hill Parker's religion remained an important part of his life. He could often be found in his room in Old East reading the New Testament in the original Greek, not in preparation for class but because of his belief that the great truths of life lay in that source. He did, in fact, give some thought to the ministry but his ambition and interest in the law steered him clear. When a fellow student, Henry Clark Smith, who later became Rector of All Saints Episcopal Church in Riverside, California tried to interest him in going on to the seminary after graduation, Parker declined saying that the law would give him "greater opportunity for growth through the constant clash with equally acute minds." Thus religion remained a private, personal element that shaped his mind in an important way, but not his career plans.

Parker's legal studies were a challenge, perhaps even a passion because the emphasis placed on fundamental principles suited the temper of his mind. His study of law was an effort to understand the great principles of life, and, in his mind, these principles were spiritual in nature. This belief, expressed so frequently in later life, that the norms and values underlying politics and government should rest on the Judeo-Christian traditions of Western civilizations was rooted in the religious teachings in his home and church.

Parker completed his law degree in 1908 and began practicing law in Greensboro in association with David Stern. Thus he began a public career that would take him to the threshold of the governor's mansion in Raleigh, the Chief Judgeship of Fourth Circuit Court of Appeals, a nomination to the United States Supreme Court, the Senior Judgeship of the United States Appellate Courts, a seat as the American Alternate Member of the International Military Tribunal in Nuremberg, Germany, and unquestioned standing as the leader of the effort to improve the administration of justice in the federal courts. It was a career that involved him in the most important constitutional controversies in the history of American Constitutional Law. Although as a federal judge he was involved in highly complex legal and constitutional issues that affected the security of the nation and the fundamental liberties of the people, his ideas about the law, the church, the family, the government and the liberties of the individual under the law did not change significantly from the patterns that were evident in his thinking during his student days at the University of North Carolina.

Cultural Heritage

Judge Parker's failures, successes and views on politics, public policy, the law, the courts and the Constitution were, of course, functions of his mental ability, character, ambitions and decisions. In an important sense, however, they were related to and derived from his cultural heritage, the place, time and circumstances of the formative years of his life. Three factors were of special importance: the qualities of his family life, the social, economic and political climate in North Carolina during the time of his youth and early manhood, and the status of race relations in the South during the same span of years.

The Parker family was no better or worse off than most working families in North Carolina and the South at the turn of the century. Times were hard; some prosperity had returned to the larger towns, but the rural areas and small towns had not really recovered from the Civil War and Reconstruction. Except among the black population, there was little feeling of being deprived or denied rights and opportunities by privileged groups in the system or the system itself. Life was tough, and the lesson was well learned that "you have to make it in this world on your own."

There were three characteristics of the Parker family that set it apart from the majority of working families in the South during that period of history: 1) a highly moralistic but unemotional church life, 2) a persistent impulse toward excellence and achievement in education, and 3) a distinguished ancestry on one side of the family that served as a model and standard of achievement for the children. Those factors bear directly on the development of Parker's character, his sense of duty, his determination to excell in everything he attempted and his general views on politics and public policy.

The Christianity that Parker learned at home and in church was not the Christianity of camp meetings and summer revivals. It was a religion of formal worship expressed through the traditional liturgy of the Episcopal faith, a religion of moral rectitude appealing more to the intellect than to emotion. For Judge Parker, religion was a sober set of principles that guided his life rather than something to preach about or set aside once the passion of acceptance had subsided. He was a theist; he believed in the existence of God as the creator of man and the world, the ultimate source of the wisdom man needed to live a civilized existence. In one sense, his was a simple faith, a straight-forward acceptance of the principles of Christianity as the foundation of his personal life. As busy a man as he was, he taught a Sunday school class most of his adult life and often spoke before Christian and Jewish groups about the relationship between man's faithfulness to religious principles and his capacity for self governance. Judge Parker's views as a federal judge on the questions of religious freedom, race relations, governmental assistance to the needy and a host of other issues concerning the relationship between people and their government were shaped by his own religious beliefs and experiences.

Judge Parker's love of books and ideas, his drive to excell at the University, his continuous and diligent study of the law and his acceptance of hard work as a duty to himself and others came out of the educational and work ethic of the Parker family. Without this drive and sense of excellence his public career would certainly have taken a different turn because no public position in the United States requires more intelligence, wisdom, intellectual discipline, knowledge of history and common sense as that of a federal appellate judge.* Appellate judges must know the history of

---

*Members of both the Circuit Courts and the Supreme Court are appellate judges.

constitutional law, the history of federal and state legislation, procedure, rules of evidence and the complexities of common law, administrative law, bankruptcy law, statutory law and equity. Furthermore, they must understand the relationships between the different branches of government, the proper functions of the various courts in the federal judiciary and the proper functions of courts of law in a democratic political process. They must make specific and binding decisions in cases and controversies that affect not only the parties in a case but also the effectiveness and legitimacy of the political system itself. These judgeships are not positions for men of merely good intelligence and modest accomplishments. Neither are they positions for men of superior intelligence who lack intellectual discipline and common sense.

Parker came to the federal bench well prepared. His native intelligence was crucial to the performance of his duties, but the key to his success was intellectual discipline and capacity for hard work. The aging process seemed not to affect him; he never lost his drive and he never settled down into a routine, comfortable existence. He moved from one challenge to the next with relish and pleasure. His work load over the course of his career was huge: his acceptance of heavy and time consuming responsibilities in the American Bar Association, service on Presidential commissions and committees and speaking engagements across the country, in addition to his work as Chief Judge of the Fourth Circuit Court, can only be explained by his sense of duty, his relish in a challenge and his pleasure in hard work. These traits were present in his character as a boy. They were nurtured and encouraged by his family life.

Many sociologists point to the family as the most important shaping force in the development of unusual talent in children. Heredity counts, but as Robert Nisbet has argued, "it is an error of vast proportion to limit this word to what is transmitted by the germ plasm. Social and cultural and moral heredity are equally real within any family line." Using Alfred North Whitehead's phrase, "the habitual vision of greatness," Nisbet stresses the importance of kinship, family ties and emulation as factors in the development of men and women of great talent. And children growing up in families where duty, honor and obligation are stressed are likely to carry these virtues into their own adult lives. Their achievements are derived, in an important sense, from the inspiration and discipline of those close to them.

Parker grew up in a family of modest means in a small country town. The extended family on his father's side, the only relatives with whom he came into contact on a regular basis, was honest and hard-working but none of its members had risen to positions of prominence and influence. But Parker certainly had a "a habitual vision of greatness" as a youth because he knew he was descended, on his mother's side, from a prominent Eastern North Carolina family that had produced two governors and a Supreme Court Justice. No bright young man, aware of his intellectual gifts, who had a natural interest in politics and law could have failed to take note of this lineage. Parker certainly did so, and concluded that he, too, could achieve success in public life if he put his talents to use. His decision to study law, his decision to enter politics immediately on completing his degree and the ambition and drive that characterized his long public career were certainly expressions of duty and obligation. But they were also related to a desire to emulate the earlier traditions of his mother's side of the family.

The careers of politicians and judges are always shaped by social, economic and political circumstances. Highly qualified people often succeed or fail because of fortuitous events over which they have no control. Mediocre people win elections or gain high public appointments simply because they happen to be in the right place at the right time. Judge Parker's public career as a politician and judge was shaped in an important way by the social, economic and political conditions in North Carolina and the South during the first thirty-five years of his life.

Politics in North Carolina during Parker's high school and college years was turbulent, bitter and heavy with racial overtones. This was the period of agrarian discontent, Populism, Fusionism, Progressivism and Republican resurgence. The Democratic party in the state at that time stood for economy in government, patriotism, conservatism and white supremacy. The Republican party, prior to the election of 1892, was little more than a "patronage ring" living off the largess of a Republican controlled White House. Around 1890 certain reformist elements in the Democratic party split away from the party and made common cause with the Populist. Following the election of 1892, the Republican party entered into a formal alliance with the Populist and created a political force that came to be known as the Fusionist Movement. In the election of 1894, supported by Republicans, dissident Democrats and a substantial number of black voters, the Fusionist ticket won control of the North Carolina General Assembly. Since the governor had no veto power, the Fusionist in the General Assembly were able to control public policy. They proceeded to return control of county government to the counties themselves, passed new election laws, fixed the interest rates on loans at six percent, increased funds to state colleges and raised the tax on property. The General Assembly elected Republicans Marion Butler and Jeter C. Pritchard to the U.S. Senate. To the dismay of the white population, and especially to the Democratic party, some blacks in the Eastern counties of the state were elected to local offices. Two years later in the election of 1896, the Fusionist gained complete control of state government by electing Republican Daniel L. Russell to the governorship.

The election of blacks to local offices in the Eastern counties and the loss of the state government to a condition of Republicans and Populists supported by the black population was more than the white people of North Carolina could accept. Racism was reintroduced into the politics of the state with a vengance. In the legislative campaign of 1898, the "Red Shirt" was waved with a new intensity. The issue in the election became "Negro control of the state." Blacks were intimidated by the charges and counter-charges and stayed away from the polls in large numbers. The Democratic party regained control of the General Assembly, and proceeded almost immediately to approve the grandfather clause amendment to the state constitution. Two years later in the gubernatorial election of 1900, which was even more racist than the previous election, black voters remained away from the polls in large numbers. Charles B. Aycock, a popular leader in the Democratic party, was elected governor and the people ratified the grandfather clause, making it a permanent part of the constitution. This amendment effectively removed fifty thousand black voters from the voting lists; this so reduced the voting strength of the Republican party that it became an insignificant force in the politics of the state. Black people were ousted from political life and one-partyism became firmly entrenched in the state. From 1900 until the mid-

1920's the Republicans held no state offices, elected only a few members to the General Assembly and captured no seats in the U. S. Congress, except for the two years period between 1908 and 1910.

During the years after 1900, while Parker was a high school student in Monroe and a student at Chapel Hill, two changes occurred in the political party system in North Carolina that were to affect his entrance into elective politics in 1908. The Republican party, deprived of its black supporters by the grandfather clause and successfully tagged by the Democrats as the party of "Negro control," again fell into the hands of a group of party leaders who were interested only in federal patronage. The reformist wing of the party, a small faction that had struggled to remake the state party in the image of the national party and make it attractive to business and commercial interest, fell into disarray. The Democrats, learning an important lesson from their defeats in 1894 and 1896, became more progressive in many areas of public policy. Professor Hugh Lefler has said of this change:

> The political revolution was highly significant for its effect upon the Democratic party. Defeated by its stubborn resistance to reform, its adherence to conservatism, and its championship of the special interests of the business classes and chastened by its experience of defeat, the Democratic party returned to power with a more useful, progressive leadership; a program of education and state development; a concern for the welfare of the common man; and a greater responsiveness to the changing needs of the state.

But the Democrats did not change their position on the issue of black participation in North Carolina politics. On this question there was no compromise.

Not much is known about Parker's political views during the years before 1908, the year he began practicing law and became active in elective politics. He was born during the second administration of Grover Cleveland, but he came of age during the Republican administrations of William McKinley and Theodore Roosevelt. His parents, most of the people in Monroe and at the University in Chapel Hill were Democrats. Parker also thought of himself as a Democrat but, according to his brother, "John admired the Republican Presidents in Washington and believed their economic policies were good for the country." As a student in Chapel Hill, he was an independent spirit who went his own way. And one of the first things he did when he arrived in Greensboro to practice law was to join the Republican party. As soon as he did this and became active in the congressional campaign of 1908, he became involved in the party controversies raging in the state. It was a decision that would change his life.

Race relations was a constant factor in Parker's public career from its beginning in 1908 until its end in 1958. He could not escape the issue; it was an important element in his three campaigns for elective office in North Carolina; it was one of the decisive forces that prevented him from gaining a seat on the U. S. Supreme Court in 1930; and it proved to be the most controversial issue he had to face as a federal judge during the last ten years of his life. As a North Carolina politician he was repeatedly accused of trying to turn the state over to "Negro control;" as a nominee to the Supreme Court he was branded as a racist who wanted to keep black people in bondage; and as an appellate court judge, duty-bound to follow Supreme Court precedents in his decisions on racial questions, he was accused of obstructing the progress of the civil rights movements.

Parker never evaded the issue; he spoke clearly and directly to every aspect of the question that came before him. There was never any doubt about what he believed personally or about his interpretation of what the law and the Constitution required. Yet, in a peculiar sense, he remained trapped in the controversy over the legal and constitutional rights of black people to participate fully in public affairs. And, whatever Parker did or said about the issue was believed to be wrong either by forces on one side of the issue or their opponents on the other.

Judge Parker lived his entire life in the South, a section of the nation where racial segregation was an integral part of the culture as well as an established fact in both ordinary and constitutional law. During his boyhood in Monroe, blacks were dependent upon whites for their livelihood. Race relations were deferential and paternalistic. Although the University of North Carolina, during Parker's five years there, was somewhat progressive by Southern standards, it was as segregated as any other Southern university at the turn of the century. Parker was not taught, either in school, church or the University, that existing laws or cultural norms were wrong. But, he was taught, and believed all his life, that all rights existing under the law could not be abridged or denied by any authority for any reason. As a practicing lawyer in Monroe from 1909 until 1922, he had many black clients, and was regarded in the town as a friend and defender of black people.

In a personal sense, Judge Parker was a friend to black people all his life. Like many other religious, educational and political leaders in the South during this period he felt only disdain and contempt for those who preached racial hatred. But he did not call for abrupt changes in the social order. On the contrary, he was suspicious of those who called for rapid and wholesale changes in American society. His views were close to those of the English philosopher Edmund Burke in this respect. Parker believed that racial barriers should and would be broken down in the United States. But this would come through the slow processes of understanding, mutual respect and a sound economy that provided jobs and a decent living standard for everybody. Society could and would be changed by education, Christian charity, individual efforts and the gradual adjustment of cultural norms to new conditions and new modes of thought.

Parker saw society as an organic entity, with laws and constitutional changes evolving out of the lives of the people. As culture changed, the laws and the Constitution would keep pace. But the key element in this process, in Parker's mind, was the quality of the nation's political leadership. Leaders who attempted to move too quickly and initiate change through laws that were unacceptable to the great majority of the people endangered public order. Conversely, leaders who were bound by the past and moved too slowly brought about the same end. Racial change had to come, but it had to come through law and at a pace that would allow a reluctant white majority to adjust and accept the new conditions whether or not they approved. Only in this way could the people's trust in the Constitution and the legal order be preserved.

Place and Time

John J. Parker became a jurist of national and international reputation, widely loved and respected by his colleagues and peers in the legal and political world. He was first and foremost an American nationalist, a man who believed that the United States was the greatest nation on earth, and the American Constitution its greatest legal accomplishment. But, he remained a North Carolinian and a Southerner and, in a personal sense, he loved these places most of all. He grew up in a modest working family in a small town during hard times, and through effort and determination, rose to prominence in the wider world. But, in a sense, he never left home. He read the *Monroe Journal,* his hometown weekly newspaper, all his life and visited his relatives in Union County whenever he had a chance. According to his son, "he believed Monroe and Union County were the best places on earth." Thus, Judge Parker remained a man in place, a man comfortable in the world but only really at home in the region of his birth, a place where so much that had to be understood never had to be explained.

John J. Parker as a young man.

II

Politics

A man who puts the welfare of his party above the welfare of his country is, in the final analysis, either a traitor or a fool.

Let us lay aside partisan prejudice and vote for political freedom and for the good of North Carolina.

Help me beat the machine.

John J. Parker

John J. Parker was active in public affairs as a lawyer, politician and federal judge from the year he finished law school in 1908 until his death in 1958. Parker was not a professional political scientist or political philosopher; he did not write books outlining his views on such esoteric subjects as the nature of politics, political man, the electoral process or democratic theory. He was a working public servant and had no time for such things, but he thought deeply about these matters. As a lawyer and politician he was concerned first with the underlying principles of political life; as a federal judge he was committed to a system of law and constitutional government that protected and preserved the principles of liberty. His views on politics were pragmatic. He was an activist, a participant; but from the beginning he was concerned first with justice and right rather than the uses of political power to gain advantage. He was ambitious and determined to achieve his goals, but never to the point of silence, compromise, or abdication of the principles that meant so much to him.

The Republican Party

Parker joined the Republican party in 1908. His friends and associates, especially those in Chapel Hill, were highly critical of this decision; they felt he had ruined his political future in North Carolina. It was a strange and surprising decision for a young man interested in elective politics in a state that was overwhelmingly Democratic in party loyalties. Why did he do it? His mother and father were Democrats, his hometown had so few Republicans that everybody knew who they were, the students and faculty at Chapel Hill were almost all Democrats, and the Democratic party was more firmly entrenched in North Carolina than at any period since the Civil War. The decision didn't make any sense, especially in light of the fact that the Republican party had been almost totally discredited.

Several explanations have been given by people who knew Parker at the time and others who knew him well later in his career. His Democratic opponents, who smarted from Parker's barbed tongue during later campaigns, gave two answers: they said he merely wanted a place at the

Republican "pie counter," a share of the patronage from the Republican administration in Washington; or that he left his father's party in a huff because Democratic leaders in Greensboro refused to pay him a fee for campaigning for the party's congressional candidate in the election of 1908. Three different explanations seem to be closer to the truth. Samuel I. Parker, John's younger brother, said that the decision reflected his agreement with the policies of the National Republican Party. Parker believed that working people had the best chance of improving themselves in a healthy and thriving economy; government regulations, therefore, should be kept at a minimum in order to allow the development of business and industry which would in turn provide good jobs and good wages. He agreed in general with the policies of the Republicans in 1908 and was very uneasy, indeed, in sharp disagreement, with William Jennings Bryan, the Democratic presidential candidate of that year.

Judge Harold Medina, a friend and judicial colleague of Parker in later years, believed that Parker's decision reflected his tendency to go his own way, to stand apart from the popular view, to distinguish himself from those who sought personal advantage from partisan affiliation. Parker was suspicious of crowds and believed that the truth was rarely found there. The third explanation was Parker's own. He made brief reference to the matter in his campaign for the governorship when he was accused of being a traitor to his father's party. He explained that it was simply a matter of principle; the Democratic party in 1908, especially the leadership at the national level, no longer stood for the principles in which he believed. He could not in good conscience continue to support a party whose principles he believed were wrong. It seems clear that Parker's decision to join the Republican party was based on national rather than state considerations, and it had to do with a basic disagreement on political principles rather than any interest in advancing his own career in North Carolina. Whatever the reason, the decision was one of the most important he ever made. It kept him out of elective office in North Carolina and eventually made him a federal judge.

Parker lost no time in becoming active in Republican politics in Greensboro. He was given a responsible position in the local party organization of the fifth congressional district and played an active role in the successful effort of John Motley Morehead to win a seat in Congress. The following year, because of the illness and death of his mother, he returned to Monroe and opened his own law office. We can only speculate about the reaction in his hometown when he returned as a Republican, but it certainly must have been one of surprise and, most likely, amusement. This sort of thing was simply not done.

The Election of 1910

In 1910, at the tender age of 25, Parker became the Republican candidate for Congress in the seventh congressional district. This district was composed of Union County and ten other counties extending from Yadkin County in the Northwestern section of the state down through the Piedmont to Scotland County along the South Carolina state line. This first effort to win elective office brought into clear focus two factors that are crucial to an understanding of Parker's political and judicial career: his association with the reformist wing of the Republican party, the "insurgents" as they were known at the time, and the mixture of race and politics that was to complicate his career until his last days.

The complete victory of the Democrats in the election of 1900 had left the Republican party in a shambles. Black voters had been disfranchised and the old wing of the party, the "pie brigade" or the "stand-patters," as it was known, was back in control and had settled down to enjoy the federal patronage. As the election of 1910 drew near, however, progressives in the party regrouped and made plans to regain control of the party. John Motley Morehead of Spray N.C., who, along with two other Republicans, had won congressional seats in 1908 much to the surprise of everyone, became the principal spokesman, planner, and organizer of this effort. Morehead had the full support of President Taft who was encouraging efforts to strengthen the party in the South and convert it into a businessman's party that would attract votes from the white middle class. To Republican leaders, this seemed the only alternative open to the party, unless it was to remain nothing more than a recipient of patronage from Washington. Blacks were out of politics and Populism had waned as a political force; thus the two elements that had produced Republican victories in 1894 and 1896 simply did not exist any longer. White voters had to be attracted to the party or it was out of business as an effective force in Southern elections.

The reformist efforts began early in the election year. Rank and file Republicans organized in almost every precinct in the state in an effort to elect their own delegates to the Republican State Convention. The objective was to oust E.C. Duncan from his posts of party chairman and national committeeman and replace him with Congressman Morehead. They were successful at the grassroots, and, by the time the Convention met in Greensboro in late summer, Morehead's victory was a foregone conclusion. Duncan, who had lost control of the local convention in his hometown of Morehead City, withdrew when it became clear that he was beaten. Morehead was elected to the party chairmanship by acclamation and, according to newspaper reports, the Republicans engaged in a "love feast." The hopes of the party, now under new and younger leadership, were high for the upcoming election.

The Republican leadership in Washington, including President Taft, considered the congressional elections in North Carolina to be of special importance. They hoped to hold on to the three seats won in 1908 in the fifth, eighth, and tenth districts and pick up new seats in the third, seventh, and ninth districts. Morehead knew that success depended on the quality of the candidates nominated. Parker, who had been nominated in the seventh district convention in Lexington just prior to the state convention in Greensboro and who had helped him win his congressional seat two years previously, was the kind of new blood needed in the party. He was a welcome member of the ticket because he was young, outspoken, and untainted by any association with the Fusionist leadership of the past and the patronage ring of E. C. Duncan. More importantly, he would be immune to Democratic charges that he would turn the state over to "Radicals and Negroes."

Thus Parker began his first campaign for political office with the full support of a state party chairman who had close ties with the President of the United States. It had to have been an exhilarating experience for a beginner, a beginner who really believed he could cast off the record and image of his party and persuade the voters of a heavily Democratic district to support him. In keeping with the new image the

Republicans had attempted to create during the state convention, Parker launched an energetic and aggresive campaign in the seventh district. His opponent was the incumbent congressman, Democrat Robert N. Page of Biscoe, N. C., who was seeking his fifth term in office. Page, who was a brother of Walter Hines Page, had a positive record in Congress and was popular all over the seventh district. He didn't expect much trouble in defeating the young attorney from Monroe.

The determination and drive so evident in Parker's character as a schoolboy and university student was clearly evident in this campaign. He set out to win. The two candidates met in pre-arranged debates in the leading towns of the district. They shared the same platform and spoke directly to each other as well as to those who came to listen. Parker got off to a poor start during the first few weeks, but, according to newspaper accounts of the debates, he improved greatly as the campaign wore on. Debating high school students in Monroe and university students at Chapel Hill was one thing; debating public policy with a four-term member of the U. S. Congress was another matter.

In this campaign Parker began speaking to a theme that he would come back to again and again in his efforts to win public office in North Carolina: the need for an active, healthy two-party system in the South. He was sensitive to the fact that the South was poor, not well-educated and far behind the rest of the country in industrial and commercial development. And he was angered by the fact that the South was viewed with a mixture of humor and disdain by many people in the United States. He wanted his home state and the rest of the South to become productive, prosperous and proud, a section that could take its rightful place in the mainstream of national life. It had the talent and capacity for hard work that could make this happen, but it was prevented from doing so by circumstances beyond its control. In his mind, two conditions, both political in nature, prevented this from happening: the almost complete dominance of the Democratic party in Southern politics and the discriminating policies of the National Republican party toward its Southern wing. The revival of an active, competitive Republican party in the South was the essential condition of any Southern renaissance.

Since this was a campaign for the U. S. Congress, Parker defended the national policies of the Republican party and pledged his support to President Taft. When the debates turned to state affairs, he defended the party's platform. The Republican platform for North Carolina called for a greater degree of local self-government, free textbooks for public school children, nonpartisan appointments of judges, and an end to bossism and machine politics. This last issue lay close to the heart of Parker's conception of political parties. He had a visceral dislike for political machines and political leaders who believed the principal purpose of a party was to win votes and gain power. His attacks on Republican party machines were no less vigorous than his repeated charges against Democratic bosses. Party rules or practices that placed power in the hands of the few at the expense of the many were anathema to him. His lifelong distaste for the patronage game as a substitute for open competition stemmed from this attitude toward organized favoritism in politics. There was a strong element of naivete in this point of view. Parker would have agreed completely with Edmund Burke on the nature of political parties. He believed them to be, or rather he wanted them very much to be, organizations based on principles of justice and right. You belonged to a party because you believed in what it stood for, not because you thought it would bring you political power. Burke's view of a political party may have made sense in the eighteenth century before the beginning of modern democratic politics, but such an elevated view could not last long in the rough-and-tumble of American elections. Parker never really abandoned this Burkean view of political parties, but in later years he accepted the fact that a political party could not survive or sustain itself if it did not appeal to the voter's self-interest and provide rewards to those who served in the ranks.

The mixture of race and politics, the second important factor in Parker's career to surface in this campaign, appeared first in state-wide contests but soon made its way into the seventh district. For the first time, Parker had to react to charges that a Republican victory would return control of the state to "Radicals and Negroes." He was faced with the "Red Shirt" tactics that had proved so effective against Republicans in the elections of 1898 and 1900. The reason the Democrats felt free to revive their old slogans was the return of Marion Butler to North Carolina. Former Senator Butler, "The Fox of Sampson County," had been the leader of the Fusionist in 1896 when the Republicans, with the support of Populist, dissident Democrats and blacks, had captured control of the state. He was literally despised by North Carolina Democrats. He returned to North Carolina in 1910 for the express purpose of helping John Motley Morehead rebuild the Republican party. Butler's speeches and appearances across the state enabled the Democrats to link any new leadership of the Republicans to the specter of black domination. They attempted to make Butler the central issue in the campaign, and they succeeded in doing so. Democratic Senator

Furnifold Simmons toured the state making speeches against Butler, calling him a traitor to North Carolina. Others charged that the entire Republican campaign was nothing more than a design to turn the state over to Butler. He was branded as a Washington lobbyist, a political adventurer, a collector of Carpetbagger bonds, and an outsider who wanted to "restore Negro domination of North Carolina politics." Senator Simmons refused to appear on the same platform with Butler who was touring the state with Vice-President James S. Sherman on behalf of Republican candidates. The *Raleigh News and Observer*, the most staunchly partisan newspaper in North Carolina at the time, referred to the Republicans as "Radicals" and said that their slogan for the campaign was, "Butler, Booze, Boodle, and Bonds."

In the seventh district race Parker could not escape the liability of Marion Butler. In fact, he did not attempt to do so; he spoke warmly of Butler as a political leader who was trying to convert the state Republican party from a patronage ring into an effective political party that would represent not the few but the many. Since he was speaking in most towns to Democrats who had come to hear Congressman Page, Parker's defense of Butler did him no good. Page used the Butler refrain against Parker with some success. And he made a charge against Parker that the Monroe attorney was to hear again and again every time he ran for public office. Page charged that young Parker was only a "pawn," a pawn of self-seeking Republican politicians like Marion Butler who wanted to rob the people of North Carolina and "turn the state government over to the Negroes."

The Republican ticket went down to defeat all over the state. Instead of winning four additional seats in Congress as planned, the party lost the three seats they had won in 1908. It was a clean sweep for the Democrats. Parker lost too, of course. But he had run a good race; with 25,000 ballots being cast in the seventh district, Parker lost by only 2,200 votes. Congressman Page, reflecting later on the campaign, said, "That young fellow from Monroe almost beat me." Given Parker's age and lack of experience and Page's incumbency and popularity, it is not likely that Parker would have won the election without the bitterness and slander. But the introduction of the old, well-worn charges about "Negro domination" and the linking of the young candidate to a sinister Republican leadership did not help. And they were to be used against him again.

Parker did not play an active role in the party strife that resumed after the defeat of 1910, but it is clear that his allegiance remained with the Morehead-Taft wing of the party that continued to work to make it more attractive to business and commercial interests in the white community. He was a member of the Republican Campaign Committee in 1912 but was not active in the struggle between the Taft and Roosevelt forces that split the national party that year. He did, however, remain in good standing with those in the party who remained loyal to President Taft. The victory of Woodrow Wilson in 1912 and the eight year reign of the Democrats that followed meant that the stakes in controlling the Republican organization in North Carolina were not very high. There was no patronage to be distributed. It was during this eight year period that Parker began to move toward a place of prominence in the state party. With a talent for debate and oratory, a record of loyalty to the party and a zest for campaigning he became especially popular among the younger elements of the party.

The Election of 1916

In 1916, with the support of Morehead, who was still chairman of the party, and Marion Butler, who was still an influential figure in its leadership ranks, Parker received the Republican nomination for Attorney General of North Carolina. This position was regarded in some quarters as the most desirable state office after the governorship because the Attorney General had to maintain many contacts across the state, and these contacts could be used as stepping stones to higher office. By this time, Parker had developed a successful law practice in Monroe and was becoming well known in legal circles around the state. His campaign, which received very little attention from the press, was conducted mainly in the defense of the party platform. This was a moderately progressive document calling for a fair election law, equitable taxation, improvement of state schools, forest preservation, agricultural education, a rural credit system and progressive labor legislation. In national affairs it demanded higher protective tariff, restrictions on immigration and an armaments program to protect the peace. *The Charlotte Observer*, the leading newspaper in the largest city in the state and only twenty-five miles from his home town, rarely mentioned Parker's name.

The statewide campaign was relatively quiet; newspaper coverage was restricted almost exclusively to the gubernatiorial race. But Marion Butler's brief reappearance in the state and increased political activity by blacks in several areas provoked the old charges of earlier elections. *The Charlotte Observer* warned that Butler was again in control of the Republican party and, as an "old friend of the Negro," would assure that "Negro votes would be

Republican votes." Repeatedly it was charged that Butler had betrayed his associates in the Democratic party, betrayed the Fusionist by leading them into the Republican party, betrayed his associates in the Republican party, and betrayed his race by sponsoring "Negro domination of the state." The Republican party was described as the unreformed and unrepentent party of Reconstruction whose record was one of disservice to the state. The standing of the Republican party in the eyes of the people was low and the revival of these old charges reduced it even more. It was not able to win votes on the strength of its stand on issues and the Democrats swept the state with their usual heavy majorities. Parker was able to muster only 400 votes out of a total vote of 2,400 in his home county of Union. He was rising in the ranks of the Republican party but moving in the opposite direction so far as winning elections was concerned.

Obtaining a place on the Republican ticket in North Carolina during these years was not difficult. The party often failed to offer a full slate of candidates because success at the polls was highly improbable, if not impossible. The main attraction for a Republican candidate was the hope of federal patronage after losing an election. The only real struggle occurring within the party involved the posts of State Chairman and National Committeeman. These were the powerful positions in the party because they controlled the state organization and the distribution of federal patronage when the National Party was in office. Nominations for statewide offices were controlled by the state organizations and party regulars were usually selected for these positions. Pre-convention contests rarely occurred and defeated candidates, except for any personal influence they might have, had no claim on places of leadership in the party. Defeated gubernatorial candidates did not become the titular leaders of the party. The Morehead wing of the party that had set out in 1910 to reform the party had not really succeeded. It was beginning to age, and after years of defeat it was becoming much like the leadership it had replaced, a patronage ring expecting defeat at home and praying for victory in Washington.

The Race for Governor

By 1920 the situation within the Republican party was beginning to change: younger, more progressive elements were beginning to increase their influence in the state organization. Morehead and others who had come to power around him were now viewed as the "old guard"; they were still in control, but their influence among the rank and file members of the party was declining. Early in 1920, Parker, now a well known figure in legal circles because of his participation in several much publicized court cases after World War I, announced that he would be a candidate for the party's nomination for governor. In February, the Republican convention in his home county endorsed his candidacy. Soon thereafter, other county conventions voted to support him and several prominent Republicans across the state declared in his favor. He was only thirty-five years old and his popularity among younger Republicans had continued to grow since his first try for public office in 1910.

When the State Convention met in Greensboro, the Monroe lawyer was clearly the favorite candidate. The Convention, proceeding with less factional strife than ever before, approved Parker's nomination by a unanimous vote. Although he was not the candidate of Morehead and the leadership of the state organization, the party factions were able to reconcile their differences, at least temporarily, and support his nomination. Morehead and the leaders of the opposing factions literally joined hands in a public display of unity. The leadership did not view Parker as a threat; he could not win and his nomination gave him no claim on power within the state organization. In their view, his nomination represented no significant change in the orientation of the party. A victory would, of course, be an entirely different matter but Morehead knew that that was not going to happen. He believed then, and said publicly later, that Parker would not carry more than 28 counties. The young man could have his fling, but nothing would change.

Parker's nomination came as no surprise. He was a tough-minded, well-spoken, successful lawyer who had been active in the party for over ten years. He was the most able and attractive young politician in the party and he had a vision of the future, not the past. In his mind, the Republican party was what he believed it to be and what he wanted it to be, not what it actually was in North Carolina at the time. He stood above and apart from the organization that he was now planning to represent to the people of the state. The new platform, and the speeches and activities that were to follow, reveal a great deal more about the candidate than they do about the party that nominated him. Parker was instrumental in the writing of the platform and that document was mainly a statement of his ideas about politics, political parties, and the responsibilities of government toward people. His acceptance speech before the convention was a point by point analysis of the platform. Expressing pride in the Republican party and declaring that leadership in a party that had been unable to win elections in North Carolina required much personal sacrifice. Parker announced the program upon which he would appeal for votes. I quote his remarks here at some length because they contain important clues to the public philosophy that shaped not only his political views but his later decisions as a federal judge:

North Carolina presents a peculiar problem because the state Democratic party by blind worship of privilege and stupid disregard of the needs of the people has fostered discontent upon which Socialism feeds. We must give the vote of North Carolina to the National Republican Party, which stands for the Constitution and the civilization of the fathers. In the state we must enact legislation and adopt policies which will remove the causes of discontent and enable us to go forward in the building of a grander and better and happier state.

It is a shame that an agricultural state has done so little for agriculture. The farmer has been asking us to revise our antiquated and unjust laws, but he has asked for bread and been given a stone. Instead of creating a new taxing system in the light of the experience of our sister states, we have revaluated the farmer's property at a time and in a manner which has aggravated the evils of the old system. I do not criticize the theory that property should be placed on the tax books at its real value. I criticize the provisions which require personal property to be listed when the merchant's shelves are empty and the farmer's barns are full. I criticize the administration of the law under which real estate has been listed not as its true value but at its inflated value due to national conditions and real estate speculation. The farmer sees that the inevitable result is to throw on his shoulders a greater share of the burden. We must have a new system. We cannot put 'old wine in new bottles,' and we cannot by patching and tinkering make a revenue system of fifty years ago meet the conditions of today.

Parker concluded his discussion of farm problems in North Carolina by calling for public assistance to young farmers and tenants in their efforts to purchase homes, obtain credit to operate their farms and some form of assistance to farmers for the storage of their crops.

He was especially concerned about the poor condition of the public schools and the poor transportation facilities available to the people:

> We have an education system under which it develops that over twenty-five percent of our young men are illiterate according to Army standards. The great state of North Carolina which pays over $200,000.00 annually in federal taxes is rich enough to lift the veil of ignorance from the minds of her children. We must have a state system of schools. We must give the boy on the country hillside the same educational advantage of the boy in Charlotte or Greensboro. We must pay our teachers higher salaries and modernize our educational methods.
>
> We must also build a state system of highways. Experience shows we cannot depend on the counties to build a state system. This system can be built by a tax on motor vehicles and gasoline and will wonderfully improve the life of the farmer and add to the commercial prosperity of the state.

In later years as a federal judge, Parker had to decide many cases in the field of labor-management relations. During the Senate debate on the confirmation of his nomination to the Supreme Court, he was branded as an enemy of labor, an enemy of the working people and a defender of exploitative capitalism. His acceptance speech shows clearly how he felt about working people, the more complicated question concerning the role of government in regulating both business corporations and labor unions, and the danger to democracy caused by clashing groups and classes that believe private interests should take precedence over the public good:

> I favor the industrial development of North Carolina. Every factory means employment for labor, investment for capital and a market for the farmer's product. The time of the anti-corporation demagogue is past. Our people and our government must give a square deal to the man who invests his money in the development of our state. Labor must be protected from the evils of the factory system. The protection of women and children, the limitation of hours of labor, insurance for the benefit of the employee against industrial casualties are too important to leave to private judgement. We must enact adequate labor legislation. Adequate labor legislation will remove the causes of industrial conflict; but when industrial conflict arises it must be met intelligently. We should not in fear destroy the rights of either labor or capital or surrender the rights of the public. Labor has the right to organize. The right to strike cannot be denied. But labor and capital have no right to fight out their differences to the danger and inconvenience of the public. The right of the public is superior to the right of any individual class. We must have a compulsory arbitration law for public service commissions, with power of investigation and mediation for other cases. The power of the state shall not be used to intimidate labor, neither shall the power of the state be withheld when necessary to uphold the majesty of the law.

After appealing for the Australian ballot, the end to election frauds and either better supervision or repeal of absentee voting, Parker turned to a discussion of what he believed to be the fundamental problem in Southern politics. Parker saw the South as a section of the country locked in the grip of "political serfdom." It was cursed by one-partyism. Southern political leadership of both parties was of low caliber because of the absence of competition, the absence of any effective challenge to its authority, and the Southern people, when discontented or dissatisfied, had no respectable alternative to the party in power. His answer to this dilemma was to revive the Republican party in the South and to increase its influence in the national party. The Democratic party would not reform itself unless it faced a real challenge at the polls, and the Republican party would never provide that challenge unless it had new leadership and could make its weight felt at the national level.

In concluding his acceptance speech, Parker brought up the question of race and politics, a question that had hung like an albatross around the neck of the Republican party in North Carolina since 1876, and to an increasing degree, around his own neck since 1910. As was his habit, he decided to face the question directly and thereby, he hoped, settle the matter so far as his gubernatorial campaign was concerned. Referring to stories already circulating in the state to the effect that the Republicans were organizing the black vote, Parker said:

> The Negro as a class does not desire to enter politics. The Republican party of North Carolina does not desire him to do so. We recognize the fact that he has not yet reached the state in his development where he can share the burden and responsibility of government. This being true, and every intelligent man in North Carolina knows that it is true, the attempt of certain petty Democratic politicians to inject the race issue into every campaign is most reprehensible. I say it deliberately, there is no more dangerous or contemptible enemy of the state than the men who for personal or political advantage will attempt to kindle the flame of racial prejudice and hatred.

Soon after the convention adjourned Parker began his campaign. In speeches throughout the state he attacked the record of the Democratic party. He demanded a new tax structure for the state, improvement of the public schools and a state-wide system of public roads. He denounced the new tax laws passed by the General Assembly which, he felt, made the farmers and home owners pay more of the government's expenses while allowing railroads and banks to pay less. He accused the Democratic administration of criminal negligence because of its neglect of the pressing needs of the ordinary working man. It would continue to neglect these needs because it was under the control of a political machine and was incapable of reform. Progressive elements within the Democratic party were incapable of influencing the party's policies.

Although Parker's speeches tended to concentrate on schools, public roads and industrial development, he also called for woman suffrage, cooperative marketing, a reduction of profits between producers and consumers, a state income tax and the creation of a state parole system. He called for the adoption of a budget system in state government, the adoption of the short ballot that would allow the governor to appoint his major department heads and the granting of the veto power to the chief executive.

Cameron Morrison, the Democratic candidate for governor, based his appeal for votes on the record of the Democratic party. He defended the new tax legislation and expressed pride in the public schools of the state. Morrison, who was later to be known as the "Good Roads Governor," did not begin discussing this subject seriously in his campaign until Parker's continued advocacy of a state-wide system of roads forced the issue. On the single occasion when the two candidates spoke from the same platform, the subject for debate was the condition of the state's roads. Speaking before the Good Roads Conference in Raleigh, Parker outlined in detail his plan for a system of public roads constructed by the state and financed by a tax on automobiles and gasoline. Morrison spoke to the group in a casual and lighthearted fashion without any reference to a specific plan for changing the existing system. According to newspaper reports of the conference, he was poorly received by the audience. Later in the campaign, Morrison charged that "young Johnny Parker and his crowd" had stolen his program for a state income tax and a state-wide road system financed by a tax on automobiles and gasoline. He then charged that Parker represented only himself and did not speak for the Republican party in North Carolina; his programs were only personal promises that would not be fulfilled by the party.

Although the principal issues discussed in the campaign were good roads, good schools, and the state's tax structure, not many weeks passed before the old issues of past elections, machine-politics and race, were injected again into the contest. The *Raleigh News and Observer*, warning that the Republican nominee was talking progress but that his party remained uncommitted to anything, declared:

> John Motley Morehead, millionaire capitalist, bosses the Republican party in North Carolina and dictated the writing of the platform. His lieutenants were careful to see that nothing committing the party to anything more than platitudes was included. Parker is a well meaning young man and doubtless thinks he speaks for the Republican party of North Carolina. Let no man be deceived by these well meaning orations by a bright young man who will be allowed to have his own way during the campaign, but if elected, would be as helpless as a newborn babe. Parker does not represent the Republican party

except as a mere figurehead. Parker will not be in the combine, of course. He has walked like a sheep to the slaughter, being perfectly willing apparently to sacrifice his ideas upon a party that has no platform, no program, except to follow the wishes of a few leaders, whose first and only thought is their own interest and how best to promote their own fortunes.

Parker, who had long been an outspoken critic of the political machine of Furnifold Simmons, retaliated in sharp tones. Speaking in Shelby, the home of O. Max Gardner, who had been defeated by Morrison in the second Democratic primary, he charged that the Simmons machine, which had backed Morrison over Gardner, was stifling the state and grinding the forward looking men of its own party to powder. The machine existed only to preserve its own interests; its reactionary policies were directly responsible for the poverty of the farmers, the retarded school system and the wretched condition of the state's transportation system. Declaring that the progressive elements in the Democratic party would never gain control of their party unless the machine was defeated at the polls, Parker pointed to his own party as a case in point:

> Roosevelt was the most powerful Republican who ever lived but he could not break the power of the machine in 1912. Kitchin was probably the most popular man in North Carolina but he dashed himself to pieces against the Simmons machine in the same year and his friends have been proscribed by the machine ever since. There is no hope for the progressive young man in the Democratic party as long as the machine is in control. If, on the other hand, I am elected, the machine will go to pieces and Gardner and the progressive younger element of the Democratic party will take charge of that party and make it stand for something other than an office-holding machine.

Nothing better ever happened to the Republican party than its defeat in 1912. That defeat killed the machine and the men in the Republican party who stand for something have come to the front. Help me beat the machine. I pledge myself not to be the governor of a faction or a party, but of the whole people. I pledge my administration to a program of constructive reforms to which every progressive citizen of North Carolina can and will subscribe. Let us lay aside partisan prejudice and vote for political freedom and for the good of North Carolina.

Parker was attacking the political machines in both parties, and calling for the end of "bossism," a fact of political life that he believed prevented progressive forces from gaining influence in North Carolina. When he said that "men in the Republican party who stand for something have come to the front," he was talking about himself. He did, indeed, stand for a set of principles; the charges that he was a party pawn, a tool of the machine, touched him to the quick. The charges and counter-charges continued. Morrison, echoing earlier Democratic charges that Marion Butler was again in control of the party and that "Republicanism and Butlerism" were one and the same thing in North Carolina, stated that the "Monroe Barrister was admittedly named by Marion Butler and rubberstamped by John Motley Morehead." Replying to this specific charge by Morrison, and to similar charges appearing in the newspapers, the "youngster," as the Democrats delighted in calling him, declared:

No, the Republican party of today is not the party of Reconstruction. It is not the party of 1896. It is a party composed of new men with new ideas. I am under obligation to no one for my nomination and will administer the governorship absolutely according to my own judgement and conscience.

In September, the explosive issue of race was introduced openly into the campaign. It had lain just below the surface throughout the year and Parker was well aware that the chances that it would come out in the election were high. Speaking in Gerrard Hall in Chapel Hill to students and townspeople several months before he received the Republican nomination, he had tried to get the issue behind him:

But what of the Negro question. Let me say this, that I believe in a square deal for the Negro. The Negro by his labor has added much wealth to the South. He has been loyal and true to his country and he is entitled to a square deal in our hands, and he shall have it. But the Negro question is not a question of politics. Experience has demonstrated that the participation of the Negro in the political life of the South is harmful to him and to the community, and is a fruitful source of that racial prejudice which works to his injury. As a class he has learned this lesson. He no longer desires to participate in politics. The Republican party of North Carolina does not desire him to participate in the politics of the state.

He failed to defuse the issue and it almost engulfed him late in September when the campaign began to grow heated. An incident occurred in Albemarle, a small town in Stanley County where the Republican party had many supporters. A white woman, supposedly by mistake, received a letter addressed to a local black woman that described Republican efforts to organize black women and to enlist their support in behalf of the Republican ticket. The newspapers picked it up immediately and dwelled at length on Republican duplicity in making pious declarations of "lily whiteism" and then at the same time trying to organize black support through the use of "secret propaganda." The Republicans cried fraud. Parker, expressing the wish to "see one election in North Carolina where it (race) was not a factor," catagorically denied any Republican responsibility in the matter. In a speech in Charlotte and also in a letter to his hometown newspaper, he explained that a Republican victory would not mean a return to black rule because "the Republican party of North Carolina is as much a white man's party as the Democratic party." We know now that Parker would have been wise to have ignored the entire issue and refuse comment because his remarks were to return to haunt him. But given the culture of the times, the record of the Republican party during Reconstruction and Fusionist period and the efforts of the party after 1910 to make itself attractive to the majority of the voters in the state, Parker's public stand on the issue is understandable. And it is in character, because as a public figure, his way was not to avoid a public issue but to face it directly.

The gubernatorial campaign of 1920 was among the most vigorously contested in the history of the state up until that time. As both the Democratic and the Republican leadership expected, the Democrats won by a safe margin of nearly 80,000 votes. Parker carried only twenty-seven counties, one less than his state chairman, John Motley Morehead, had predicted. But he amassed a total of 230,000 votes. This was the largest Republican vote ever cast in North Carolina and exceeded by nearly 63,000 votes the total number of votes ever received by a gubernatorial candidate of either party prior to that election.

Parties and Politics

If the size of the turnout and the increased support for the Republican candidate are measured against earlier elections in North Carolina, the campaign of 1920 can be viewed as a personal victory for John J. Parker. Parker had planned, organized and conducted his campaign almost single-handedly. He received little or no support from the state party organization; Morehead and the other party regulars were less active in this campaign than in any other election since 1900. Parker knew this was going to be the case; in fact, he wanted things that way because he was really trying to take over the Republican party and reform it. Had he won the governorship, there is no question but that he would have attempted to reshape the Republican party in his own image. In a modern sense, Parker was not a party man at all; he was more of an eighteenth-century figure who believed that principles, not political maneuver, should be the chief characteristic of a political party. One of his clearest statements to this effect was made in Chapel Hill during the campaign:

> Political parties are but associations of men having the common purpose to incorporate certain principles or policies into the life of the state. They are entitled to support only so long as they represent the principles in which we believe; when they fail to represent these principles, we owe it to ourselves to support a party which does represent them. In laying this down as a principle of action, I am stating no mere academic position but the rule upon which I have not hesitated to act myself. I have been criticized by certain shallow-minded persons because, upon attaining manhood, I did not support

the party which my father supported. One of the things in my life of which I am proud is the fact that in 1908, when the Democratic party nominated Mr. Bryan and adopted a platform in which I could not believe, God Almighty gave me the courage to do my duty as I saw it. And I stand ready to part company with the Republican party if it ever repudiates the principles in which I believe. I think with Curtis that an American citizen should 'carry his sovereignty under his own hat.' A man who puts the welfare of his party above the welfare of his country, is, in the final analysis, either a traitor or a fool.

Apart from the question of race, and on this issue he must be judged by the cultural norms and political realities of the times, Parker conducted the most progressive state-wide campaign in the history of North Carolina up until that time. He called for significant changes in state government and political parties that would open the system to greater participation; he called for the expansion of government services to assist needy people; he called for a system of politics that placed the public welfare above the interests of groups and classes; and he insisted that the principles of justice and right rather than power should be both the means and ends of politics.

Three factors were present in Parker's campaign for governor that help explain his politics. First, his strong commitment to the place of principles in political and public life. This quality of mind, which was evident in his makeup during the student days in Chapel Hill, shaped his policy positions and appeal for votes. It literally rang in his speeches; he was not just spouting rhetoric, he believed what he was saying. Parker seemed to speak from some inner sense of duty that compelled him to say exactly what he meant. This is not to suggest, of course, that he was

always right, because he was not. But the duty to do the right thing rather than the expedient thing was a strong force acting on his political decisions. In later years when trying to lead his court to a decision in an important case he said, "nothing is ever settled until it is settled right."

This sense of duty, this compulsion to do the right thing in public affairs was, I think, a religious impulse. Although his entire life was devoted to politics and public affairs, this part of his nature was not rooted in the law, the Constitution or the ordinary affairs of man. It had much to do with his belief in God, his belief that the world and the people in the world had been created by a force greater than man. Man's first duty, whatever his profession or station in life, was to serve God and to live his life according to the great principles found in the traditions of the church. Parker believed that democracy, as it had taken shape in America, was based upon a set of great principles that were religious in nature. Although he was an Episcopalian and his view of life was essentially Christian, he was not a sectarian in any sense of the word. His belief that political life should reflect religious principles was simply a conviction that there was a natural order of things, created by God, and politics should adhere closely to those fundamental principles that underlie all of life.

A second factor, perhaps the most important factor, in understanding Parker's politics was his belief in the welfare, dignity, and liberty of the ordinary working man. His concern did not spring from some ideology, theory or intellectual dogma that placed the "workers" above all others in the social order. Indeed, such schemes were totally foreign to his mind. He did not view working people as a "class," and the last thing he would have accepted is the view that some historical imperative was at work in the lives

of men to place one class over another. Parker cared for the plain people because he was one of them. His family and neighbors were working people and he loved them all. His speeches in 1920 are filled with references to the ordinary Americans: farmers, mill-workers, teachers, and people who struggled to get by. Parker called for government policies to provide opportunities that would allow the common man to take care of himself. The proper function of government, and one of its most important functions, was to protect the people from political and economic oppression caused by the selfish manipulation of the rich and powerful or by the government itself. He did not think of economic and social classes as legitimate actors in the political process; a political process based on class conflict and struggle was, in his mind, one of the greatest threats to democracy. And nothing provoked him quite so much as politicians who catered to this kind of thinking. He wanted to preserve an open society in which people, free from unfair restraints and oppressive conditions beyond their control, could develop themselves, make their way up the economic ladder and accept responsibility for their own lives.

This belief in the liberty of the individual and the need for government to stay out of his way explains Parker's lifelong distaste for collectivist politics. In 1920 he had not worked out any elaborate brief against class politics and the erection of a huge service state. But he saw the dangers of both intuitively. He knew that conflict was inherent in politics; but he also knew that democratic politics in the long run must rest on a harmonious community. But this community must come into being through education, religion, love and charity; it could not be created by law and maintained by administrative restraints. Parker's criticism of his own party's narrow views and his charges that the

Democratic party, despite its claims to the contrary, neglected the common man were based on his conviction that lack of opportunity for the ordinary working people would create the "discontent upon which socialism breeds." He may not have been correct so far as the Democratic party was concerned, but his principle was sound; it points to social and economic hardship as the key factor in making people susceptible to the appeals of collective politics. Perhaps Parker's most fundamental belief was that the most important function of government, other than protecting the security of the nation, was to create and preserve conditions that allowed the common people, through work, the use of their talents and the exercise of their liberty, to get ahead in life. A political process that favored the few over the many, that set one class against another, that substituted administrative decisions for individual choice, that honored security more than freedom and neglected the need for timely reform was a process alien to what Parker believed to be wise, sensible and democratic.

The participation of blacks in elective politics was the third factor in the election of 1920 that reveals something of Parker's view of politics. In a word, Parker became trapped on this issue. He could not escape history — the history of his home place, his state, region, political party and his times. Parker was a friend to blacks on a personal basis. As a politician he defended their right to participate in elective politics as individuals according to existing law, and later, as a federal judge, he would brook no violation of their rights under established interpretations of the Constitution. In the election Parker did not say that individual blacks should not vote or that they should not vote for Republican candidates. He simply defended himself against the "Red Shirt" campaign of the Democrats and the charges that his party was attempting to organize black citizens as a class, a voting bloc in politics. Parker believed, given the hostility toward blacks in North Carolina at the time, that any such effort would increase the level of racial prejudice in the community and make life more difficult for individual blacks already voting for candidates of their choice. To condemn him for not calling for repeal of the grandfather clause and other restrictions on black participation in politics is to judge him by the standards of our own time rather than his own.

Parker's views on the participation of blacks in politics and public life were consistent throughout his public career. These views were derived from his more fundamental views on social and political change and the role to be played in these changes by custom, religion, law and the Constitution. He paid the penalty in full for this consistency; as a politician he was castigated by his opponents as an ambitious Republican who wanted to return the state of North Carolina to "Negro domination"; as a federal judge he was branded as an unregenerated Southern racist who wanted to keep American blacks in bondage. The irony is clear and the explanation is simple. Those who opposed Parker as a politician and those who disliked his decisions as a federal judge did not listen to what he said or read his decisions carefully. Both charges were wrong, clearly at odds with the public record. They were based on what his detractors wanted to believe about him rather than anything he ever believed, said, or did in regard to the question of race and politics.

The election of 1920 marks both the high point and the end of John J. Parker's career in elective politics. He was a man who pushed to the front, and if a position of leadership was denied him, he would move on to other things. His defeat showed clearly that political leadership in North

Carolina was most likely beyond his reach. Back in 1908 his friends had been correct; changing political parties had closed the doors to high political office in his home state. And he had no interest in playing routine partisan games at the local level. In 1922 he accepted a position as senior partner in a successful law firm in Charlotte and moved there to expand his practice of law. In the same year he refused to allow his name to be considered for the position of Republican National Committeeman and in 1924 rejected all efforts to persuade him to seek the governorship again. He did consent to accept the position of National Committeeman that year out of a feeling of party loyalty and because control of patronage had been removed from that official.

Parker had never had any interest in routine party work and he found the patronage game distasteful. But he was no longer naive about patronage; his experience had taught him its importance in the life of a political party. And he had come to believe that in the South, where Republicans could not win elective office, they should be appointed to as many high federal offices as possible in order to retain some semblance of balance in local and state affairs. Thus his interests in Republican politics at the national level remained high and he continued to be involved. This involvement in a different phase of politics, the politics of the judiciary, would make him a federal judge.

III

Politics and The Judiciary

Having allowed myself to get in the position of being considered for the place, I naturally want to be appointed, but whether I am appointed or not, I don't think I will ever allow myself to get in such a position again.

                                        John J. Parker, 1925

Congratulations! I look forward with the greatest pleasure to our collaboration.

                    Chief Justice Charles Evans Hughes, 1930

I want to see men put on the Supreme Court who have modern ideas and who are not so encrusted with ancient theories which existed in barbarous times that they are going to inflict human slavery upon us now.

                        Senator George W. Norris, 1930

"To the victor belongs the spoils" is not just a slogan; it is part and parcel of the American game of politics. As a young politician in North Carolina, John J. Parker was opposed to the politics of patronage; he saw the distribution of jobs as the main currency of political machines. And "bossism" was, in his mind, the single most significant feature of the stagnant politics of his home state. As he gained experience in trying to reform and rebuild his own party he developed a better understanding of this aspect of politics, but he never felt comfortable about it and avoided any participation in the handing out of favors. But, he took a more sanguine view of patronage after his defeat in 1920, especially regarding the selection of federal judges:

> I know that in the appointment of judges political considerations should play little part, and yet in this state where all of the judges of the state are elected by the Democratic party which commands a majority of the voters, I think the fair administration of justice is best preserved by the appointment of Republican lawyers to the federal bench.

Parker made this statement in 1922, the year he became senior partner in the Charlotte law firm of Steward, MacRae and Bobbitt. He was the only Republican in the firm and was its youngest member except one. He had grown weary of elective politics and had turned his mind and energies toward the practice of law. His invitation to move to Charlotte as a head of a well established law firm was due to his standing as an attorney and had little to do with his leadership in the Republican party. When his friends in the party urged him to allow his name to be considered for a federal district judgeship that was becoming vacant he refused:

As a matter of fact, I do not think I would want to accept the judgeship under any circumstances... it might lead to advancement in the judiciary, but I must confess the more I think about the judgeship, the further I am from desiring it .... I am afraid that I am temperamentally unfit for a judgeship. I feel quite certain that I would not be a good trial judge.

The federal district courts may well be the most important courts in the federal judiciary, but they are local trial courts at the bottom of the judicial system where judges preside over adversary proceedings and juries determine guilt or innocence. District judges are the workhorses of the system and their responsibilities are important, but they are mainly involved in the application of the law according to interpretations made by other judges above them. Important as these courts are, district judgeships are not leadership positions in the federal judiciary. Parker knew himself well and his lack of interests in a district judgeship was completely in character. There would be no real and lasting challenge, no real "opportunity for growth through the constant clash with equally acute minds," to recall one of his remarks as a university student.

Appointment to the Fourth Circuit Court

When an appellate court judgeship became vacant on the Fourth Circuit Court in Richmond, Parker took a different view of the matter. The federal appellate courts are not trial courts; taking cases from the district courts on appeal they deal with matters of law and constitutional interpretation in the same manner as the Supreme Court. Appellate court judges hear cases from a much broader area of the nation, five states in the case of the Fourth Circuit Court, and the challenges are more scholarly and philosophical than is usually the case in the district courts. The work is essentially the same as that of the Supreme Court except that appellate court judges do not have final authority in determining the meaning of the Constitution. An appellate court judgeship is certainly no automatic stepping-stone to the Supreme Court, but it is a high honor, worthy of any ambitious lawyer whatever his ultimate goals in life. There is no doubt that Parker wanted this nomination from the moment the vacancy became known to the public.

Competition for the seat was quiet but keen, and developed into what was essentially a political struggle between Republican forces in three states — North Carolina, Maryland, and West Virginia. Parker's name was urged on President Coolidge by many public figures from both political parties in North Carolina and South Carolina. Parker did not want "to appear in any sense as a candidate for the position," but he became deeply involved in mustering support for his candidacy in North and South Carolina. His public reticence and private pressures were merely maneuvers in the well established process of judicial appointments. Two things were clear to Parker: the nomination would go to a Republican lawyer who had served the cause of the party, and it would come to him if the President chose someone from the Southern end of the Fourth Circuit. Parker was the front-runner in the Southern end of the Circuit because he was clearly the most able Republican lawyer in the two-state area with a strong party record. Although the contest was mainly a Republican affair, the efforts in behalf of Parker were bi-partisan. His friends in both parties, his law partners and Parker himself made a quiet and successful effort to discourage other candidates and to unite as many people as possible in North and South Carolina behind him.

Parker's competition came from the northern tier of states in the Circuit, mainly West Virginia. West Virginia had two Republican Senators and they, along with other politicians in the state, were putting strong pressure on the President. Parker, writing to friends in Washington, made the best case for his own nomination. He pointed out the Maryland and Virginia were already represented on the Fourth Circuit Court, therefore the vacant seat should be filled from one of the other three states in the Circuit. If the appointment went to West Virginia, it would mean that all three appellate judges would be residents of the northern end of the Circuit. Furthermore, Maryland, Virginia and West Virginia were common law states; it would be wise, sensible and practical to appoint a lawyer from North Carolina or South Carolina both of which were code law states. Parker put a fine point on his argument with a reminder that Judge Woods, who had just vacated the seat, was from South Carolina; therefore, it was North Carolina's turn to be represented on the Circuit Court. Given Parker's standing in the legal fraternity and his record of party service, the argument that the appointment should go to North Carolina was a straight-forward brief for his own case.

The effort to win the nomination for Parker was a quiet but full-fledged campaign involving lawyers, politicians and judges from both political parties. The case was pressed to the point in Washington that Parker supporters in North Carolina were advised that any further activity would jeopardize the appointment. The campaign was conducted through letters and private discussions; it did not become a highly publicized affair because an appellate judgeship was in question, not a seat on the Supreme Court. Parker was fully involved in the effort and it could well have been his logical analysis of the need for regional balance on the Circuit Court that tilted the decision his way. He did not enjoy his involvement in the campaign; it brought him dangerously close, and he knew it, to the old Republican patronage game that he had always opposed. But, his involvement and his actions were in character: to pursue a goal, once selected, with all the energy and facilities at his command. He indicated, before the decision was finally made, that he was not inclined ever to get mixed up in such an affair again.

Parker was nominated on October 2, 1925, and the nomination was confirmed by the Senate as a routine matter. The appointment was well received in North Carolina because Parker had been endorsed by prominent figures in both political parties. Democratic leaders had supported him because they knew that no member of their own party would receive the appointment and the Charlotte lawyer's qualifications for the position could not really be seriously questioned. But, there was one exception: Parker's old nemesis, *The Raleigh News and Observer*. Observing that federal appointments in North Carolina went first to party regulars who had served their apprenticeships in hopeless elections, the editor concluded:

> The new circuit judge came to his high judicial position by playing the game of Republican politics in the accepted style of the South...the new circuit judge had been part and parcel of the Republican pie-counter brigade in North Carolina and has at all times played the game as the pie-counter brigade wanted it played. He had manifested none of the characteristics of an outstanding leader though the opportunity has come to him more than once to stand up in his own right as a leader.

The appointment, of course, was political because the process of staffing the federal courts is itself political. Parker's service to the Republican party was a key factor in his candidacy for the nomination, but the decision was not made on that basis. He received the nomination because he was highly qualified and because of the strong bi-partisan support he received in North and South Carolina. And the logic of appointing a judge from the Southern tier of the Circuit was unassailable. The *News and Observer's* charge about the old Republican pie-brigade and its low estimate of Parker's legal and judicial abilities was merely a restatement of the newspaper's old refrain voiced so consistently and frequently during the partisan strife of an earlier day. As a general rule, judicial appointments below the Supreme Court level are not matters of serious dispute unless unqualified candidates are appointed. In Parker's case, with the exception of the sour note from Raleigh, there were few if any objections concerning the legal qualifications of the President's choice.

Nomination to the Supreme Court*

When Supreme Court Justice Edward T. Sanford died in 1930 the usual speculation about his successor began. Mr. Justice Sanford was a Southern Republican and conventional wisdom suggested that President Hoover would fill his place with another Republican from the same

---

*This discussion of the Supreme Court nomination in 1930 is a revision of my article, "The Senate Rejects a Judge: A Study of the John J. Parker Case," Political Studies Program — Research Report No. 3 (Chapel Hill: Department of Political Science, University of North Carolina, 1962).

section of the country. As is always the case, the list of names of prominent lawyers and judges suggested to the President was long. Judge Parker's name was on the list. With five years of judicial experience, he had become Acting Chief Judge of the Fourth Circuit and, in addition to supervising the federal courts in a five state area, had written more than 125 opinions. In legal circles and among the judges of the Fourth Circuit, Parker's opinions were recognized as the work of a superior judicial mind.

Following Mr. Justice Sanford's funeral the pressure on the President to nominate Judge Parker increased, as did efforts to persuade him to choose other well qualified candidates. Delegations of citizens from North Carolina and the Southeast called at the White House, prominent members of bar associations and many judges in the lower federal courts testified by letter and telegram to Parker's outstanding qualifications, ten Southern Democratic senators and seven Democratic governors contacted President Hoover in Parker's behalf and the two Democratic senators from North Carolina soon joined in the effort. The North Carolina senators had first recommended the nomination of Chief Justice W. P. Stacey of the North Carolina Supreme Court, an old school mate of Parker's at Chapel Hill, but soon abandoned this effort because they knew that a Republican would receive the nomination.

North Carolina Republicans were, of course, more anxious than any other group to obtain Parker's nomination and in guarded moves joined the campaign. The effort on behalf of Parker in Washington was lead by North Carolina Republican Congressman Charles A. Jonas. In a letter to Parker he explained the approach that had to be taken: "We must avoid any political color. The matter must be handled in a dignified non-partisan manner because too much political color will hurt. The bar and judiciary should lead in the drive to get the nomination." This time Parker stayed well clear of the efforts to influence the President's decision. He was not just a Republican lawyer, he was now the Acting Chief Judge of the United States Court of Appeals, Fourth Circuit. He maintained contact with Congressman Jonas and wrote short letters of appreciation to those who had publically endorsed him for the nomination. But he avoided any comment on the pending decision or any contact with any officials involved in the matter.

After a thorough investigation of Judge Parker's record and a review of his judicial opinions, the Attorney General recommended him to the President as a federal judge of great distinction and high competence, fully qualified for the position for which he was being considered. Newspaper reports then suggested that Parker would most likely be the President's choice. On March 10, 1930, President Hoover made his decision and sent Parker's name to the Senate for confirmation, a decision everyone involved in the question thought would be a routine matter. Chances for confirmation were high: Parker's appointment would provide balance to the Court, it would give representation to the Fourth Circuit Court which had not had a Supreme Court Justice since the Civil War, Parker was clearly well qualified by virtue of his education and judicial experience, and he had strong bi-partisan support in his home region and the rest of the country. When the President's decision was made public, there were no dissenting voices. Parker's office in Charlotte was literally inundated by congratulatory messages from prominent political and judicial figures of both political faiths. The Hoover Administration looked upon Parker as a nominal Republican of moderately conservative persuasion whose record as a federal judge was invulnerable to criticism. The nomination appeared to be a good one and no difficulty was expected even though token opposition from the growing liberal forces in the Senate was a possibility.

The Committee Hearings

Senator Lee Overman, Democrat of North Carolina, served as chairman of the subcommittee of the Senate Judiciary Committee appointed to study Parker's nomination. His colleagues on the sub-committee were Senator William E. Borah, Republican of Idaho and Senator Felix Hebert, Republican of Rhode Island. On March 24, Overman wrote to Parker that he was not planning to hold a hearing on the nomination because only one minor objection had been raised. Overman indicated that all members of the subcommittee would support the nomination and the general feeling in Washington was that the matter was settled. Chief Justice Charles Evans Hughes wrote to Judge Parker, "Congratulations, I look forward with the greatest pleasure to our collaboration."

The one minor objection, however, proved not to be minor at all. The American Federation of Labor announced that it was opposed to Parker's appointment because of an opinion he had written in a court case between the United Mine Workers and the Red Jacket Coal Company of West Virginia. President William Green of the AFL sent word to Overman that he wished to appear before the subcommittee and make a statement. Overman then changed his mind and scheduled open hearings on the nomination. He informed Parker of these developments and indicated that the opposition of the AFL would most likely lead to some opposition in the full committee. By April 5, the day the subcommittee opened its hearings, the protest initiated by the AFL was gaining momentum; letters and telegrams began descending on members of the subcommittee and on influential members of the Senate. The situation was becoming confused and the climate was beginning to change. The charges of the AFL against Parker were being carried in newspapers across the country.

Senator Overman opened the hearings by introducing a long series of letters and newspaper editorials urging confirmation. He reviewed Parker's credentials in detail and submitted elaborately prepared memoranda answering the objections raised by the AFL. Following Overman's remarks, Green introduced an official statement protesting the appointment of Parker and urging the Senate to reject the nomination. The circumstances giving rise to the AFL objection are crucial to an understanding of the increasing opposition to Parker and the change in climate in the Senate that led eventually to his defeat.

On April 18, 1927, Judge Parker had handed down a decision in the case of *International Organization, United Mine Workers of America* v. *The Red Jacket Consolidated Coal and Coke Co.* He had upheld an injuction issued by a federal district court against the United Mine Workers that prevented any interference by the union in the operations of certain coal mines in West Virginia. The case had grown out of the unrest and violence stemming from efforts of the United Mine Workers to organize employees in non-union mines in the early 1920's. Many of these mines were operating under closed-non-union shop agreements, commonly referred to as "yellow-dog contracts." The district court's injunction prevented any further effort on the part of the unions to attempt to persuade, peaceably or otherwise, the employees working under such contracts to join the unions in violation of these contracts. In upholding this injunction, Judge Parker, speaking for the Fourth Circuit Court of Appeals, based his decision on a Supreme Court precedent established in the case of *Hitchman Coal and Coke Co.* v. *Mitchel*, decided in 1917. The facts were the same; in the *Hitchman* case the Supreme Court had upheld the validity of yellow-dog contracts. The United Mine Workers had challenged the jurisdiction of the federal courts in the *Red Jacket* case, but Parker had ruled against them citing as precedent the Supreme Court's decision, in the second case of *Coronade Coal Co.* v. *United Mine of America* handed down only two years previously in 1925. After Parker's decision, the Supreme Court refused to hear the case on appeal and the decision against the United Mine Workers became final.

The AFL's opposition to Parker was based squarely on his decision in the *Red Jacket* case to uphold the injunction against the United Mine Workers. Speaking to the three members of the subcommittee, Green argued that the members of the Supreme Court of the United States should possess a "trained mind, sympathetic toward the hopes and aspirations of the masses of the people as well as a knowledge and understanding of modern day economic questions and human relations in industry." Judge Parker, he continued, did not have these qualifications and that labor opposed him because of his judicial attitude and point of view regarding economic and industrial problems facing the nation. Green then denounced yellow-dog contracts at great length, decried the inhuman effects of Parker's decision and spelled out what he thought would be the results for the country if the nomination were confirmed:

The significance is not that Judge Parker followed the precedent of the *Hitchman* case but that his opinion reflects a judicial attitude entirely in sympathy and accord with the legal and economic policy embodied in the injunction. Confirmation will mean another 'injunction' judge will become a member of the Supreme Court. The power of reaction will be strengthened and the broadminded, humane, progressive influence so courageously and patriotically exercised by the minority members of the highest judicial tribunal in the land will be correspondingly weakened.

At one point in his remarks Green claimed that Judge Parker was wrong and that the facts in the two cases were different, but he did not dwell on this point. He stressed the view that Judge Parker should have expressed a reluctance to follow the Supreme Court precedent even though he felt bound to do so. He reviewed the facts in the *Red Jacket* case and then stated that Parker had not in fact followed the precedent established in the *Hitchman* case:

It is perfectly apparent that Judge Parker has gone far beyond the doctrine laid down by the Supreme Court of the United States and that he has, in effect, practically stated the law to be that it is unlawful, by any means whatsoever (even though there is no element of violence, threat, fraud or deceit) to endeavor to induce or persuade an employee to join a union if such employee is working under an alternative agreement hereinbefore described and generally known as a 'yellow-dog' contract.

In concluding, Green stated that although he knew nothing of Parker's record as a citizen or a man that indicated an unfriendly attitude toward labor, he also saw nothing in his record that indicated outstanding legal ability. Moreover, Parker had lived in a narrow, provincial environment, had limited experience and was not well-informed about modern-day economic problems. Green's presentation made little or no impression on Overman and Hebert, but it did impress Senator Borah. He was very interested in Green's view about Parker's judicial attitude in general and about yellow-dog contracts in particular. After Green had concluded his remarks, Borah said that "the gist of the matter was that the injunction was issued against union men trying to persuade non-union men to break an illegal contract."

Although Overman expected only one protest against Parker to be presented to the subcommittee, two more objections were raised, one in the form of a letter and the other from a witness who wanted to testify. The letter was from Norman Thomas, Chairman of the Committee on Public Affairs of the Socialist Party. Thomas' objections to Parker were essentially the same as those lodged by the AFL. He concluded his letter by saying, "a great judge fit for the bench at this critical time, if he could not find a way around precedent would have found a way to dissociate himself from apparent moral approval of it."

E.C. Townsend, counsel for the United Mine Workers in the *Red Jacket* case, was then called to testify in Judge Parker's behalf. Under sharp questioning from Senator Borah, Townsend pointed out that the validity of the yellow-dog contracts was not even an issue before Judge Parker's court; their validity had been established in the *Hitchman* case and that he, as counsel for the labor union, knew from the very beginning that Judge Parker was bound by that precedent. He stated that he knew nothing in Parker's record that indicated an unfriendly attitude toward labor. He concluded by saying, "I do not think the decision of Judge Parker in this case, according to my idea of it, is sufficient to warrant his disapproval as a member of the Supreme Court of the United States." Green, at this point, objected to Townsend's testimony and said, "He does not speak for anyone connected with the AFL— he is not with us — we do not agree with him." Senator Borah questioned Townsend at length on the question of Parker's alleged anti-labor attitude and attempted to determine whether or not Parker, if confirmed, would be a reactionary judge and continue to support the legal status of yellow-dog contracts.

As the subcommittee prepared to conclude its business and adjourn, one last witness, who had not officially requested to be placed on the agenda, asked to be heard. Walter White, Secretary of the National Association for the Advancement of Colored People, then submitted a statement made by Judge Parker when he was seeking the Republican nomination for governor of North Carolina in 1920:

> The Republican Party of North Carolina has accepted the [literacy test and grandfather clause] amendment [to the North Carolina Constitution] in the spirit in which it was passed and the negro has so accepted it. I have attended every state convention since 1908 and I have never seen a negro delegate in any convention that I attended. The negro as a class does not desire to enter politics. The Republican party of North Carolina does not desire him to do so. We recognize the fact that he has not yet reached the stage in his development where he can share the burden and responsibility of government. This being true, and every intelligent man in North Carolina knows it is true, the attempt of certain petty Democratic politicians to inject the race issue into every campaign is most reprehensible. I say it deliberately, there is no more dangerous or contemptible enemy of the state than the men who for personal or political advantage will attempt to kindle the flame of racial prejudice and hatred.

White informed the subcommittee that he had sent a telegram to Judge Parker inquiring about his present views on the question of blacks participating in politics but had received no reply. The NAACP assumed, therefore, that Parker's attitude had not changed during the ten years since his statement had appeared in the press:

> Parker cannot approach similar questions with that dispassionate, unprejudiced and judicial frame of mind which would enable him to render a decision in accordance with the federal constitution. No man who entertains such ideas of utter disregard of integral parts of the federal constitution is fit to occupy a place on the bench of the United States Supreme Court.
>
> With the economic, educational and political progress which the Negro is making and with the growing consciousness of the part of intelligent Americans as to the importance of the settlement of the race problem upon a basis of evenhanded justice, it seems probable that even more cases under the 14th and 15th amendments will be presented to the Supreme Court for decision.

It would be improper, White concluded, to place such a man as Parker on the Supreme Court because of the kind of cases that would be coming before the Court in the near future. Under questioning from Senator Borah, White stated that he knew nothing in the career of Judge Parker to indicate an unfriendly or unjust attitude toward black people except the one statement that had been submitted to the subcommittee. White concluded his testimony with this statement: "Frankly, we had never heard of him until he was nominated by President Hoover and the only part of his record we have studied is this one statement upon which we base our objection."

The hearings of the subcommittee ended on this note. The meeting had been brief, lasting only about four hours. The report to the Senate Judiciary Committee was two to one in favor of confirmation. Senator Borah, who, according to

Senator Overman, had favored confirmation before the hearings began, cast the one negative vote. Judge Parker remained in North Carolina well clear of the controversy that was beginning to surround his appointment. Senator Overman had advised him to make no public comments on the charges lodged against him unless he was officially asked to do so.

By April 5, with the opposition of both the AFL and the NAACP officially registered and the opposition of Senator Borah reported in the press, the Parker supporters were still not seriously concerned about the fate of the nomination in the Senate. By April 15, however, a campaign against Parker, organized mainly by the NAACP, was well underway. Congressman Jonas and Senator Overman began to understand the significance of the forces that were marshalling against the nominee. The chances of confirmation seemed to be deteriorating each day as charge after charge was levied against Parker. Congressman Jonas addressed a long letter to Senator Joseph T. Robinson of Indiana, who was reported to be under strong pressure from black constituents, refuting all the charges against Parker. By April 18, Jonas had become so concerned that he sent copies of his letter to Robinson to every member of the Senate. At this point, he realized that the dangers to the confirmation were very real and that Parker, if he hoped to win in the Senate, would have to come to his own defense. The leader of the anti-Parker effort was now the NAACP; the AFL, other labor groups and the Socialist party had stepped aside in favor of the black organization. At this stage of the struggle, Parker was not really vulnerable on the question of yellow-dog contracts. He had merely followed the precedents of the Supreme Court which he was duty-bound to do, and he had refused to comment on the wisdom or correctness of these precedents which he was also duty-bound, as an appellate court judge, not to do. No lawyer, judge or informed politician would have taken issue with him on either count so long as that was the only charge against him. But, the racial question was another matter entirely; he was vulnerable there. The labor organizations thus stood aside during this period just before the Judiciary Committee was scheduled to consider the nomination because the racial argument was better suited to achieve the ends both opponents were seeking.

The Judiciary Committee, chaired by Republican George Norris of Nebraska, met on April 21 to consider the nomination. There are no records of the discussions, but Senator Overman reported that the session was long and heated. When the charges made by the AFL and NAACP were submitted to the full committee, Overman introduced a motion to allow Judge Parker to appear before the Committee to answer the charges against him. The motion was voted down, and the Committee made its decision without hearing Parker in person or reading any explanations that he had written himself. The vote was ten to six against confirmation. Four Republicans and two Democrats voted in favor of confirmation; six Republicans and four Democrats voted against confirmation. All ten of the negative votes, including the Republican Chariman, George Norris, were cast by senators from the Mid-West and West; all the affirmative votes except one were cast by senators from the East. When the adverse committee vote was made public, several newspapers, including the *New Leader*, a Socialist journal in New York City reported that Parker's nomination was now in deep trouble because of the racial question. The protest of the NAACP was believed to be the key reason for the negative votes of the Republican members of the committee.

By April 24, three days after the announcement of the committee report, nothing had been heard from Charlotte, no indication that Judge Parker was going to reply to the charges made against him. Senator James Watson, the Republican floor leader in the Senate, wrote to one of Parker's supporters:

> Confidentially, the way the matter stands right now, he is whipped in this fight. The prejudice against him is intense and a small ember has been fanned into a great flame by the Negro opposition in those states where that particular vote is strong.

Parker's fortunes were indeed declining because the contest being conducted in the public press was one-sided; the news reports were dominated by the accusations against him and contained no reports of his explanations because he had made none. And, since he had not been allowed to testify before the committee, very few senators had had any personal contact with him. His silence led to charges that he was a "weakling and an unknown," and this gave some credence to the views of his opponents who argued that he was unqualified for the position. Immediately after the announcement of the adverse committee report, Judge Parker broke his silence and issued public denials of all the charges made against him. These denials were in the form of carefully prepared statements concerning his decision in the *Red Jacket* case and his political speeches about racial questions during his campaign for governor in 1920.

The Senate Debates

The Senate began formal consideration of the nomination on April 28. Early in the session Senator

Overman presented Judge Parker's official statements concerning the accusations that had been made against him both in the hearings of the subcommittee and the full committee. Parker's first statement tried to clear up the confusion about the *Red Jacket* case, and his duty in deciding the case as he did:

> I followed the law laid down by the Supreme Court and will not elaborate upon it. This is the duty of the lower courts and any other course would result in chaos. The "yellow-dog" contract was upheld in *Coppage* v. *Kansas* in 1914 and again in the Hitchman case in 1917. I had no latitude or discretion in expressing any opinion or views of my own but was bound by these decisions to reach the conclusion and render the decision that I did. The appeal in the *Red Jacket* case did not contest the validity of the contracts or the scope of the injunction. The principal point pressed related to the jurisdiction of the court, but this was clearly controlled by the decision in the second Coronado case. The Red Jacket case is much misunderstood. The injunction did not prevent employees from quitting work or joining a union.

We know now that Judge Parker took too lightly the charges of the American Federation of Labor. He was firm in his regard for judicial ethics and procedure and, from his first days as a judge, he had refused to comment publicly on cases before his court. His brief statement to the Senate was in character on this point. Most likely, Parker felt that nothing further needed to be added. The issue in the case was perfectly clear; the duties and restraints of an appellate court judge were also clear. No sound or reasonable case could really be made against him on this point. What Parker apparently did not fully appreciate was that his value system and attitude was under attack, not just his decision in one court case. He had not been allowed to testify before the

Judiciary Committee and he had no personal contact with those senators who were beginning to accept the view, repeated often in the press, that he was an "injunction judge" who had no sympathy for the plight of the laboring man in a depressed economy. Under the best of circumstances, a defense against such a charge would have been difficult to prepare and use effectively. And it was exactly that charge that was to become an increasingly important element in the campaign against the nomination.

Judge Parker's reply to the charges of the NAACP was also brief and to the point, but he did try to speak more directly to his attitudes on this question:

> The fear of the Negro is entirely groundless. I regard the constitution and all its amendments as the fundamental and supreme law of the land and I deem it the first duty of a judge to give full scope and effect to all of their provisions. In the discharge of my duties as a circuit judge, I have never hesitated, I hope and believe, to meet this obligation in the fullest degree. The effort to interpret some statements alleged to have been made ten (10) years go in a speech in a political campaign as indicating a contrary disposition is wholly unjustified. My effort then was to answer those who were seeking to inject the race issue into the campaign under a charge that the Republican party of North Carolina intended to organize the colored people and restore the conditions of the Reconstruction era. I know the baneful effect of such a campaign and sought to avoid it. The charges against me are untrue and entirely misrepresent my attitude. I endeavored to conduct my campaign for governor on a high plane and with fairness to all classes of the people; and while I made it clear that my party was not seeking to organize the colored people as a class, I, at no time, advocated denying them the right to participate in the election in cases where they were qualified to do so, nor did I advocate denying them any other of their rights under the constitution and the laws of the United States. In

conclusion, let me say that I have no prejudice whatever against the colored people and no disposition to deny them any of their rights or privileges under the constitution and the laws. I think that my record as a judge of the United States circuit court of appeals, on a circuit where many of them reside, shows that I have no such prejudice or disposition.

At 3:00 o'clock the Senate prepared to begin debating the question of Judge Parker's confirmation as a Supreme Court Justice. At this point, Senator Overman asked for the unanimous consent of the Senate to postpone any discussion of the question for several days until Senator Furnifold Simmons, Democrat of North Carolina, could be present on the floor. Senator Borah would not agree to this delay so the debates began as scheduled. The debate, which was long, repetitive, bitter and unruly, continued until May 7. Overman began the debate by reviewing Parker's qualifications and then pointed an accusing finger at Senator Borah calling him "the laboring oar in this contest because of his persistent and adverse attitude toward the confirmation." After retorts by Senators David Walsh, Burton K. Wheeler and George Norris, Senator Hugo Black of Alabama injected a new issue into the discussion.

Black quoted an editorial from a Scripps-Howard newspaper (one of the few newspapers in the country that opposed Parker) that charged Judge Parker with improper conduct during a trial he had handled for the government before he became a judge. According to the editorial, Parker, while serving as a government prosecutor in the lumber fraud cases after World War I, had withheld evidence that would have cleared the man he was trying to convict. Black then stated that he would vote against Parker unless the allegation was disproved. After Overman again defended Parker, Senator Thaddeus Caraway, Democrat of Arkansas remarked:

It is strange that this extraordinary lawyer who possesses
all the virtue and all the character attributed to him was so
unknown. How he ever concealed all these virtues I have
never been able to find out.

Senator Borah then launched a long and biting attack on
Parker that was not concluded until the following day. His
address consisted of a long denunciation of yellow-dog
contracts and a detailed dissection of Parker's decision in the
Red Jacket case. Borah's principal point was that Judge
Parker was in error in depending on the precedent of the
Hitchman case because, according to his reading of
constitutional law, the *Hitchman* case had been overruled by
a later decision of the Supreme Court. When Borah had
finished, Overman introduced a series of letters from
interested lawyers, as well as the presiding judge in the
lumber fraud cases, that clearly refuted the charges made
earlier in the debate by Senator Black. Several senators
spoke to the faulty reasoning Borah had used in his
discussion of the *Red Jacket* case and then Senator Clarence
Dill of Washington made a remark that showed how
differently he viewed the functions of an appellate judge
compared with the views held by the judges themselves. He
said that Parker's failure to register dissent from a precedent
he was duty bound to follow disqualified him to sit on the
Supreme Court.

At this point in the debate, several new issues were
introduced into the controversy. Senator Simeon Fess of
Ohio delivered a long speech supporting the nomination and
concluded with a line of reasoning that was to prove to be
significant in understanding the ultimate outcome of the
contest. According to Fess, Parker was not the issue at all;
he had become an "incidental" in a much larger and more

significant issue — the survival of the Supreme Court as an arbiter of the Constitution free of partisan or political predispositions. Fess saw the opposition to Parker as a crusade by labor groups, the NAACP and certain members of the Senate itself "to break down the American judiciary." Fess knew, of course, as every other member of the Senate knew, that no American court is ever free of predispositions. His point was that the efforts to defeat Parker had very little to do with either the record or legal qualifications of the North Carolina judge. The objective was to reshape the philosophical complexion of the Supreme Court by denying a seat to a lower federal court judge whose views on political and economic questions were not entirely clear and whose views on the law clearly showed a firm belief in the value of established precedents.

Senator Henry Ashurst, Democrat of Arizona, speaking for the first time, then levied one of the few direct and open attacks on the professional qualifications of the nominee. He called Judge Parker a weakling with no great character, capabilities or experience. At a later point in the debate, Ashurst extended his attack by charging that President Hoover's nomination of Parker was purely a political act, a clear effort to strengthen the Republican party in North Carolina. The senators, now lining up against Parker, made much of Ashurst's charge of "pure politics." Their suspicions on this point were strengthened by the appearance of an item that came to be known as the "Dixon letter." This letter had been written to President Hoover urging the nomination of Parker and indicating that such a move would be a "master political stroke." Although the Dixon letter was only one of hundreds of endorsements of Parker that made no mention of Republican politics, it proved to be a useful piece of correspondence for those who were working against confirmation.

On April 30, the third day of the debate, several other senators joined in the discussion. Senator Daniel Hastings of Delaware spoke at length in support of the nomination. He accused Senator Borah and the other outspoken opponents of Parker of being primarily interested in putting men on the Court who agreed with their own social and economic ideas. Hastings urged the Senate to consider the nomination as a matter of principle and to make its decision on that basis rather than caving in to the whims of pressure groups. The only other major speeches made that day were by Robert F. Wagner of New York and Kenneth McKellar of Tennessee. Senator Wagner's remarks were essentially the same as those of Senator Borah, except that the New Yorker placed much greater emphasis on the racial question. Senator McKellar covered the same ground but concluded that Parker lacked independence of mind and would be a "me too judge."

On May 1 the debates were again repetitious, with no new issues being raised either for or against Parker. Senator Henry Allen of Kansas spoke for the first time and urged the Senate to confirm Judge Parker. In an exchange between Allen and George Norris, the Chairman of the Judiciary Committee and an ardent opponent of Parker, the Nebraska senator said:

> I am frank to admit that I want to see men put on the Supreme Bench who have modern ideas and who are not so encrusted with ancient theories which existed in barbarous times that they are going to inflict human slavery upon us now.

Senator Allen replied, "By modern ideas you mean your own ideas." Senator Norris answered, "I do, of course, mean my own ideas."

Senator Norris was the principal speaker on May 2. The dominant theme in his address was a plea for "more humanity on the court." Then Norris spoke to a point that until this time had not been seriously stressed in the the debates. After extended remarks about the quality and bent of Judge Parker's mind, he charged that the North Carolina judge had only one idea, "big business, wealth, and the virtue of large aggregations of wealth." The senator concluded, "Mr. President, I close as I began. Judge Parker is only an incident. The Supreme Court is only an incident. Human liberty is the issue. The preservation of our government is the issue." Emotional charges of this nature tend to stick like glue in heated debates where feelings are running high. They are difficult to refute, especially among wavering senators who do not know the person in question and have only written statements before them. After Norris' speech, Senator Furnifold Simmons, Democrat of North Carolina, who had finally arrived in the Senate, introduced a statement by the North Carolina Bar Association endorsing Parker and urging his confirmation.

The debates on May 5 added nothing new to the arguments of the previous week, except a bit more emphasis on the political nature of the appointment. Attorney General William Mitchell's statement explaining the reasons for President Hoover's choice were read into the *Congressional Record*, and this statement indicated that Hoover had rejected efforts of some Republican senators to get him to withdraw Parker's name from consideration. The President had chosen to stand behind his nominee. Senator Hubert Stephens of Mississippi spoke in behalf of Parker for the first time and appealed to his fellow Southerners to support the nomination. He quoted from an editorial in the *Baltimore*

Sun that pointed out that if the opposition forces succeeded in defeating Judge Parker it would mean that any other Southerner nominated to the Supreme Court would receive the same treatment. Senator Ashurst, who had earlier attacked Parker personally, then gained the floor and charged that certain senators were being offered bribes in the form of federal judgeships if they would support Parker. Repeating his earlier charges, he said that "Parker lacks judicial ability, lacks courage, lacks talent, lacks training, and the appointment was purely political." These charges that members of the Senate were being bribed, and Ashurst's implication that Judge Parker was in some way involved, created quite a disturbance and further poisoned the atmosphere in the Senate.

When debate resumed the following day, May 6, Senator Carter Glass of Virginia called for an investigation to determine the truth or falsity of Ashurst's accusations. After a heated discussion, Senator James Watson, the Republican leader in the Senate, joined the debate for the first time. He moved that Ashurst's charges be referred to the Judiciary Committee for investigation. Finally, after an explanation from Senator Dill, who seems to have been the source of Ashurst's information, the Senate realized that the charges were groundless and the matter was not discussed again. Ashurst made one last effort against Parker by calling for an investigation by the lobby committee of Parker supporters who were putting pressure on some members of the Senate to support the nominee. No action was taken on this request and, after several more speeches both for and against the nomination, the Senate agreed to vote on the question the next day.

Defeat

The following afternoon, May 7, 1930, with the gallery filled to capacity and with members of the House of Representatives standing three-deep in the aisles of the chamber, the Senate voted 41 to 39 to reject the nomination of Judge Parker to be an Associate Justice of the United States Supreme Court. It was a tense moment as the Parker supporters awaited the votes of their colleagues who were believed to be in favor of Judge Parker but were known to have weakened under pressure from those opposing the nomination. Seventeen Republicans, twenty-three Democrats and one Farmer-Laborite cast their votes against the nomination. Twenty-nine Republicans and ten Democrats voted to confirm the President's nominee. There were eight pairs. This was the first time since 1894 that a Presidential nomination to the Supreme Court had been rejected by the Senate and would not occur again until Clement J. Haynsworth, who was also Chief Judge of the Fourth Circuit Court of Appeals, was rejected by a vote of 55 to 45 in 1969.

The rejection of Judge Parker must be viewed as an extraordinary event in the politics of judicial appointments because Parker was the only Supreme Court nominee rejected over a span of seventy-five years. And these were unusually turbulent years because of the changes occurring in American social, economic and political life. But his defeat was not a unique event; rejections had occurred before and they were to occur again. Prior to 1894, Senate rejection of Supreme Court nominees was not uncommon; approximately one fifth of these nominations went down to defeat. This is not surprising; nominations were made for partisan reasons, and the Senate reacted to them the same way. After 1894, this emphasis on partisan politics gave way to broader concerns about social and economic attitudes. When Senate debates on a Supreme Court nominee are essentially partisan, and the senators know this to be the case, the issue remains rather simple. Tempers may flare and charges exchanged but there is little doubt about the reasons for the outcome. But when ideology becomes the key issue, the nature of the controversy changes because ulterior motives are not always apparent: minor weaknesses of the nominee are exaggerated, human failures are denounced as perversities, isolated actions or words are seen as revelations of fundamental mental traits or temperament and fair evaluation gives way to full-blown rhetoric and bombast.

Judge Parker was not the first Supreme Court nominee after the turn of the century to face this kind of situation. Louis Brandeis was almost defeated in 1916 because of the conservative opposition, but Harlan Fiske Stone, who was nominated in 1925, was the first nominee to face the kind of opposition that defeated Judge Parker. The liberal opposition was strong but was able to muster only six votes against him. By February 1930, just three months before Parker's turn came, these same forces were able to cast twenty-six votes against Charles Evans Hughes who had been named to the Chief Justiceship. Hughes, who had served on the Supreme Court from 1910 until 1916, was nearly sixty-eight years old and his tenure on the Court would not be long. By this time, the Senate had adopted a new rule that required presidential nominations to be considered in open executive session unless otherwise provided for by a majority vote. This made it possible for outside forces to play a much greater role in the fight over the nominations of Hughes and Parker than had been the case with earlier nominees. Hughes, as a former Justice, former Republican Presidential candidate in 1916, and a highly respected and well-known national figure, was not spared any criticism of his alleged ideological leanings. Senator Borah, who had voted for Stone, played a leading role in the fight to defeat Hughes just as he was to do three months later in the rejection of Parker. Judge Parker was not a national figure and he was only forty-five years old. If confirmed he could serve on the Court for thirty years and this was viewed as a serious threat by the liberal forces in the Senate.

The change of one vote in the Senate would have put Judge Parker on the Supreme Court; the count would have been even and the Vice President would have supported the President's nomination. What happened? Who beat Parker? In the weeks following the Senate vote, newspaper editors attempted to analyze the situation and award either credit or blame to one single force or factor. Technically, every senator who voted against Parker could take credit for his defeat and every group working against him in the campaign outside the Senate could do the same. But the truth of the matter is that no single group or person defeated Judge Parker. The North Carolina Republican became a victim of a peculiar set of historical forces at play in American politics at the time.

The first, but perhaps the least significant, factor in the defeat was the opposition of the American Federation of Labor. Even a cursory reading of materials and decisions having to do with Parker's attitudes on labor-management relations or the problems of working people shows that the arguments of the labor forces are untenable. The arguments of Senators Borah, Wagner, Norris and McKellar concerning the *Red Jacket* case were merely weapons used against the nominee. Few if any senator accepted them as an acceptable refutation of the legal soundness of the judge's decision. But labor did influence the votes of Senator Black of Alabama, Trammell of Florida, Connally of Texas and Carraway of Arkansas. This is surprising in view of the weakness of organized labor in the South at the time. In Ohio, Pennsylvania, New Jersey and West Virginia, where labor spoke with a stronger voice, all eight senators voted for confirmation. And labor opposition declined noticeably after the question of race was introduced into the controversy. But the voice of labor must be given some weight because it contributed to the general clamor surrounding the nomination in the early stages when little opposition was expected.

A second factor was the charges levied by the National Association for the Advancement of Colored People. When the Parker nomination was announced, the New York office of this organization wired contacts in North Carolina inquiring about Parker's record and his attitude on the race question. One black official remembered the statement made by Parker in the campaign of 1920 and sent a newspaper article containing this statement to the New York office. With this statement in hand, the NAACP, under the leadership of Walter White, launched its campaign against the nomination. With the Baltimore *Afro-American* setting the pace, such black weeklies as the *Boston Chronicle, Chicago Bee, Chicago Defender, Oklahoma City Black Dispatch* and the *Cleveland Gazette* denounced Parker because of his racial views. By May 7, the day of the Senate vote, only two of over two-hundred black newspapers in the country had not taken a firm stand against placing the North Carolina judge on the Supreme Court. Had Judge Parker replied immediately to White's telegram asking for clarification of remarks quoted in the Newspaper in 1920, this growing opposition might have been partially diffused. But he chose not to reply. This was a serious mistake, no matter that it was consistent with Parker's resolve not to become involved in a public debate about his appointment before the committees of the Senate began their deliberations. When Judge Parker's official statements were finally made public, after the adverse vote in the Judiciary Committee, black leaders gathered in Washington in a "peace conference" to consider withdrawing their objections. According to the *Washington Post,* Walter White personally prevented this group from changing their position, and then "took to the country where he beat the bushes of Negro feeling with all the gusto of an Anti-Saloon League expert."

After the Senate vote, the NAACP claimed credit for Parker's rejection. Its efforts were general in nature and were aimed at the entire Senate, but it was especially heavy on senators from states where blacks were voting in significant numbers. Black leaders believed that their effort had changed ten votes. Their efforts had been concentrated on senators from Massachusetts, New York, New Jersey, Pennsylvania, Maryland, Ohio, Indiana, Illinois, Michigan, Kentucky and Tennessee. Of the twenty-two senators from these states, thirteen voted against confirmation. Eight of these senators faced reelection in 1931 or 1933. President Hoover says in his *Memoirs* that when the pressure from the NAACP mounted, several Republican senators "ran like white mice." Three senators to whom Hoover was referring, Charles Deneen, Otis Glenn and Arthur Vandenberg, were specifically asked by the President to support the nomination. They refused to do so for fear of defeat in future elections. Only Senator Deneen, however, was facing an election in the near future.

The NAACP did not rest on its laurels after the vote on Judge Parker. White began a campaign of retribution against those senators, especially in New Jersey, Pennsylvania and Ohio, who had disregarded the pledge of the NAACP to defeat them if they voted the wrong way:

> If the Negroes are to be respected and their demands heeded, we must make good on the threats we made during the fight against Parker. If we fail in our promised retribution on the Senators who voted to seat him, we will possess as little prestige as the AFL whose pleas, threats and demands always have gone unheeded.

The NAACP then distributed a list of all senators, their dates of reelection, their stand on the Parker nomination and instructions as to which ones to support and which ones to oppose. White added: "Any Negro is a traitor to the race who votes for a Senator who voted for Parker."

Although we do not know exactly which senators changed their votes because of pressure from the NAACP, there can be no doubt that the opposition of this organization was an important factor in changing the odds against Judge Parker. The *Washington Post* observed that the Parker fight represented the first significant stirring of a black organization on the national level. Prior to this struggle, black efforts to shape the course of politics had either been ineffective or restricted to local events. Oswald Garrison Villard saw the same significance in the efforts of the NAACP: "The Negroes for the first time since Reconstruction have demonstrated to the entire country that they propose to use their political power hereafter in safeguarding their rights." Participation in the defeat of Judge Parker did indicate a greater degree of cohesion and political muscle on the part of black organizations; it increased the prestige and standing of the NAACP and "put that organization on the map as a protagonist of Negro rights."

A third factor, partisan politics, was certainly at play on the Senate floor. Twenty-three Democrats opposed the nomination; ten of these were Southerners. The senators from North Carolina, Virginia, Louisiana, Mississippi, South Carolina and one senator from Florida supported Parker. All other Southern senators voted against him. They were roundly condemned by Southern newspaper editors for opposing Judge Parker for the sole reason of obstructing any growth of the Republican party in the South. Six Democrats from the mid-Atlantic and Northeastern states opposed Parker, most likely because of the race question and the remaining seven Democrats were all from the Western states, the home base of the progressive Republicans who led the fight against confirmation.

Length of service and seniority in the Senate also may have had something to do with the way the votes fell. There was no pattern of committee concentration; that is, no committee had a noticeably larger proportion of its members voting either one way or the other, except the Judiciary Committee that issued the adverse report. And, of the thirty-three committee chairmen (Republicans) in the Senate, nineteen supported Judge Parker, and of the seventeen different senior minority members of these committees (Democrats) only eight supported the nominee. Thus the older members of the Senate split about even on the nomination. But Parker didn't fare nearly as well among those senators with limited tenure. Of the twenty-six senators who had entered the Senate between 1925 and 1927, nineteen voted against confirmation. Thus approximately forty-eight percent of the negative votes came from senators who had been in the Senate less than one full term. If brief tenure suggests a greater sensitivity to the constituents back home, then it seems clear that the junior status of these nineteen senators was a factor in the outcome. The most important factor in Parker's defeat was the opposition of the progressive Republicans from the Western states. Of the forty-eight votes cast by senators from the West, thirty-six were against Parker and twenty-nine of these were Republican votes. The situation was almost exactly the reverse in the East where thirty-four votes were cast for Parker and only fourteen against him. If the Mississippi River is taken as a rough dividing line, the rejection of Judge Parker takes on a definite Western coloration. Taking all things into consideration, it is clear that from the very beginning, the day the subcommittee held hearings on the nomination, if trouble was going to develop, it would be from the progressive wing of Parker's own party. Senator Overman informed Parker soon after his nomination that he might be opposed by "11 or 12 Radicals," but no more than that. Overman was referring, of course, to the same senators who had opposed the confirmation of Chief Justice Hughes.

If any senator or senators can be singled out as keeping Judge Parker off the Supreme Court it has to be Senators Borah and Norris. Borah cast the one negative vote in the subcommittee and Norris was chairman of the full committee that refused to let Parker testify in his own case and then filed an adverse report on his nomination. This refusal to meet and talk with Judge Parker personally and the negative recommendation to the Senate gave the upper hand to those who opposed the nomination early in the contest. Borah and Norris led the opposition on the floor of the Senate and made the most inflammatory speeches. Their efforts to brand Parker as the father of the yellow-dog contract and to impugn his record as a federal judge was merely a tactic. The legal reasoning of these two senators, along with Senator Wagner, concerning the *Red Jacket* case has been described as "scrambled eggs." Although wise men differ on matters of law, it is difficult to believe that either Borah or Norris believed what they were saying. They were determined to keep Parker off the Supreme Court and they simply adopted methods they believed would succeed.

The fight to defeat Judge Parker was in the final analysis an ideological struggle in the eyes of those who opposed him. Senators Borah and Norris saw Parker as a Southern conservative who would take a reactionary view of social and political change. Had they talked with him personally, read all his campaign speeches of 1920 rather than just the statement on race, studied his judicial decisions or sought the opinions of people in North Carolina who knew him, they might have been persuaded to a different point of view. Republicans in North Carolina had never thought of Parker as a conservative and President Hoover did not hold that view of him when the nomination was made. And Judge Parker certainly did not hold that view of himself. No one was more surprised than he when he learned of the labels that were being affixed to his name.

Borah and Norris wanted to reserve the vacant seat on the Supreme Court for someone more in tune with their own ideas on social and economic policy. Senator Norris admitted this freely and openly when he replied to Senator Allen's question about the meaning of modern ideas: "I do, of course, mean my own ideas." The fact that no one was really surprised by Norris' remark is instructive; there was no surprise because there was nothing to be surprised about. Ideology had always been a part of the politics of judicial appointments. But it is more important in some periods than in others, and in the twentieth century it has become increasingly central to both the appointment and confirmation phases of the process.

The vote cast in the Senate on May 7, 1930, was not a vote on John J. Parker at all; it was merely a small skirmish in a much larger political struggle over the proper functions of government in a changing society. Judge Parker was only an "incidental," a casualty in the head-long rush of four groups to gain objectives that were more important to them than a fair and balanced evaluation of a relatively unknown federal judge. The progressives, both Republicans and Democrats, wanted to change the complexion of the Supreme Court which they believed to be reactionary in its views of the law; the NAACP wanted to reserve the vacant seat on the Court for a justice with no ties to Southern politics and, more importantly, it wanted to show its strength as a political force in the country; the AFL wanted to register its continued disapproval of the legal validity of yellow-dog contracts and judges who enforced them; and a number of Democrats simply could not bring themselves to support an appointment they believed was really a move to strengthen the Republican party in the South, the most solidly Democratic area of the country and a firm base of party support.

Politics and Judicial Appointments

Judge Parker was deeply disappointed by his defeat. His greatest ambition at this point in his life was to become a Justice of the Supreme Court, and to lose this opportunity because of emotional charges that were unfounded and untrue must have been difficult to take. To be branded as a racist and reactionary on the floor of the Senate was not only painful but insulting. But, Parker accepted all of this without bitterness or rancor; he made no public comment, either at the time or at any later time, on the content of the Senate debates or the outcome of the vote. He understood the political nature of the process in which he was involved and that time and circumstance had as much to do with success as qualification for office. Judge Parker fully expected to be nominated again and to be confirmed by the Senate. He resisted efforts from friends to persuade him to return to the private practice of law or re-enter North Carolina politics and run for the Senate himself. He was not interested in making money and his earlier zest for elective politics was gone. Also, he was not willing to campaign against those North Carolina Democrats who had given him such strong and loyal support during the fight over the Supreme Court nomination. More importantly, during the five years on the Fourth Circuit Court Parker had found his true calling: he was no longer a lawyer and politician, he was a judge:

> My appointment by the President, even though not confirmed, will probably give me an outstanding position as a circuit judge and will cause my opinions to be more carefully scrutinized than they would otherwise be. It is my hope, therefore, that I may develop as a judge and that My opinions may aid in the development of the law and in the solutions of the problems with which the country is faced.

Judge Parker was correct in his belief about the effect of the nomination; the nature of the charges against him and the closeness of the vote made him a nationally known figure.

His opinions were read more carefully and his contributions to the development of the law are now recognized. But he was wrong in his belief that he would receive another nomination to the Supreme Court; the politics of the process of judicial appointments was simply against him. From 1930 until 1956 almost every time a vacancy occurred on the Supreme Court, Parker's name was put before the President. There were two principal reasons for this prolonged effort in his behalf: the view held in many quarters that experienced federal judges should be advanced to the Supreme Court and Parker stood at the top of the list; and the general belief in judicial and legal circles, and in political circles after his decisions on New Deal legislation, that Parker had been so unfairly treated by the Senate in 1930 that the country had a moral obligation to make things right. During the 1930's many senators publicly expressed their regret in having voted against Parker and wanted a chance to redeem themselves by voting for his confirmation on another occasion. Although Parker's name was presented to the White House every time a vacancy occurred during this long twenty-six year period, serious efforts were made to gain a nomination on only three occasions: the resignation of James C. McReynolds in 1941, the resignation of James F. Burns in 1942 and the resignation of Owen J. Roberts in 1945.

Between 1933 and 1940, President Franklin D. Roosevelt appointed five new Justices to the Supreme Court: Hugo Black, who had helped defeat Parker in the Senate, in 1937, Stanley F. Reed in 1938, Felix Frankfurter in 1939, William O. Douglas in 1939, and Frank Murphy in 1940. All were Democrats and, by this time, Judge Parker had accepted the fact that he was out of the running because if President Roosevelt had any intention of nominating a

Republican, he would have named him to one of these vacancies. He thanked his friends and supporters for their confidence and continued efforts in his behalf, but his optimism about another nomination was gone. Judges, lawyers and other prominent figures from across the country were among his supporters, but the most direct and persistent pressure on the White House came from North Carolina Democrats.

During the period prior to the nomination of Justice Murphy, O. Max Gardner, a former Democratic governor of North Carolina and a prominent Washington lawyer and lobbyist who was a close friend and advisor to President Roosevelt, contacted the President personally and urged him to name Parker to the post. Gardner told Roosevelt that "the injustice of 1930 must not stand." Roosevelt agreed that Parker was "the outstanding Republican of judical timber in this country," and the only one he had in mind "if called upon to make an appointment to this high office." Roosevelt agreed that "Parker had been done a great wrong in 1930" and told Gardner that he could not nominate another Democrat after he named Murphy. Gardner felt, and so informed Judge Parker, that he was next in line for the Court and that Justice McReynolds would soon be resigning.

When Justice McReynolds stepped down in 1941, Gardner led a serious but quiet campaign, supported by Frank Graham, President of the University of North Carolina and other prominent figures, to gain the seat for Judge Parker. Parker was no longer a young appellate court judge; he was Chief Judge of the Fourth Court of Appeals and nationally known jurist because of his leadership in the American Bar Association to reform the federal judiciary and improve the administration of justice in both the federal and state courts. More importantly, he was known as a "New Deal judge" who had upheld the constitutionality of several important pieces of New Deal legislation and then had his decisions reversed and struck down by a conservative Supreme Court. Parker also had much support from newspapers and other groups in the country that believed the time had come to name an "honest-to-goodness" jurist to the Supreme Court. None of Roosevelt's appointments at that time had had any judicial experience except Justice Murphy who had filled a minor court position early in his career. In the opinion of many people, both Republicans and Democrats, "it was time for a real judge" to be seated on the Court.

Parker, of course, was interested in the effort being made in his behalf and stated to a friend that he "might have a fair chance," but he was not optimistic about the sincerity of President Roosevelt's remarks to Gardner the previous year. Rumors were circulating in Washington that Senator James F. Byrnes of South Carolina wanted the appointment and that if he wanted it he would get it. Parker knew that Byrnes was a close friend to whom the President owed many obligations and that his chances, therefore, were not good. He wrote to a friend, "I am inclined to think that the situation is such that there is not much that can be done..." As the signs pointed increasingly to the nomination of the South Carolina Democrat, Gardner wrote to Parker:

> We cannot meet expediency or promises based upon matters over which we have no control. I shall never give up my sincere determination to live to see you on the Supreme Court and in this view I am absolutely firm.

The appointment went to Senator Byrnes.

When Justice Byrnes resigned from the Court after only one year's service, the supporters of Judge Parker renewed their efforts. This time they felt, more intensely than in previous years, that the South, the Fourth Circuit and Judge Parker had a rightful claim on the seat. Gardner and Graham continued their efforts and were joined by many others. Gerald W. Johnson, an influential liberal journalist with deep family roots in North Carolina, urged Roosevelt to appoint Parker, pointing out to the President that Parker as a North Carolina politician had "decontaminated the Republican party in 1920." George Rossman, Associate Justice of the Oregon Supreme Court, wrote to the President:

> Contrary to our wishes, jurisprudence does not produce many men of outstanding merit. It produces many good men who are fair, earnest and competent; but the very nature of our science, depending much upon precedent and the doctrine of *stare decisis*, has a strong tendency to keep all our thinking in the same groove. Generally, we reject rather than welcome a fresh point of view. Judge Parker is one of those rare individuals on the bench who is capable of originality and who has achieved an improved outlook. He sees the result which the law aims to achieve....

There were no ideological problems so far as Judge Parker was concerned; his decisions on New Deal legislation were in the public record and anyone keeping abreast of the developments in constitutional law knew about them. President Roosevelt certainly knew about them; the problem was clearly one of partisan politics in the White House. Judge Parker knew this; he did not discourage his friends but he knew his chances of being named by Roosevelt were very slim. But he did feel, perhaps more strongly than most because he was a careful and thoughtful student of the judicial process, that the Supreme Court badly needed balance and, more importantly, it needed a jurist who had had much experience in the lower federal courts. These judges needed some assurance that Supreme Court seats were not reserved for politicians and professors. Concerning the question of balance, he wrote, in a sense of resignation:

> The Fourth Circuit composed of Maryland, Virginia, West Virginia, North Carolina and South Carolina has not had a representative on the Court since the death of Chief Justice Taney in the sixties, except the period of about a year served by Mr. Justice Byrnes. There has not been a North Carolinian on the Court since the death of Mr.Justice Moore in 1804.

The appointment went to Judge Wiley Rutledge of the United States Court of Appeals, Washington, D. C. Rutledge, a Mid-Westerner, had been a law professor and dean and had had four years' experience as a federal judge. He was a Democrat and a long-time supporter of the New Deal.

When Justice Owen Roberts, who had been named to the Court in 1930 after Parker's defeat, retired in 1945 one last sustained effort to gain an appointment for Parker was made. Senator Clyde R. Hoey, Democrat of North Carolina, was a prominent supporter of Parker and urged President Harry Truman to make the nomination. Judge Parker was now one of the most widely known and respected appellate court judges in the country. Although sixty years of age, he was in robust health and at the peak of his career. His name was a household word in judicial and legal circles because of his New Deal decisions, his many speeches across the country, articles in law journals and the almost continuous speculation about a much deserved Supreme Court nomination. And, just two years earlier he had written an opinion in *Barnette* v. *West Virginia State Board of Education.* In this controversial and much publicized case, Parker had held unconstitutional state laws requiring public school students to salute the flag. He had deliberately and knowingly departed from a clear and controlling Supreme Court precedent in the area of religious freedom. The Supreme Court upheld Parker on appeal, but he received a sharp rebuke from Justice Frankfurter upholding the right of the state to require flag salutes.

This last major attempt to gain a nomination for Judge Parker rested on several considerations: a continuing determination that the wrong of 1930 had to be made right, a belief that it was long past time for the Fourth Circuit to be represented on the court, repeated assertions that the Supreme Court had become the special preserve of politicians and law professors and that John J. Parker was the best qualified and most deserving federal judge in the country. The dissension and bitterness among the Justices of the Supreme Court during that period was believed to stem from the clash of personalities and different philosophies; the appointment of an experienced and widely respected jurist was seen as a step toward the solution of these problems. Justice Rossmann of the Oregon Supreme Court, who had supported Parker in earlier efforts, did so again and shared this opinion with Parker:

> Seemingly each appointment is carrying the Supreme Court farther away from the legal profession and making it more akin to the administrative bodies. The constant neglect of judges who have served faithfully in the lower courts and the preferment for senators and law school deans should be a concern of the American Bar Association.

During the course of events the press reported that President Truman had shortened his list of candidates to four names. Judge Parker was one of the four. When this became known, one of the charges that had defeated Parker in 1930 was injected into the discussions. The *Baltimore Afro-American* stated in an editorial that "we are not yet convinced that the leopard had changed his spots... what change there is is due to his association with Judge Soper and Judge Dobie." Soper and Dobie were Parker's colleagues on the Fourth Circuit Court. Judge Soper contacted Carl Murphy, the editor of the paper, and discussed the editorial. After this discussion, the *Afro-American* printed no more statements critical of Judge Parker. There is no record of what Judge Soper said to the editor. Most likely he referred him to some of Parker's opinions, for example, *City of Richmond* v. *Deans* and *Alston* v. *School Board of City of Norfolk,* cases in which Parker had struck down state action discriminating against blacks.

Although Parker was one of the last four names under consideration, the odds were never good that he would get the nomination. This was President Truman's first appointment and it was believed that he would name someone he knew, and most likely someone from his own section of the country. Judge Parker certainly realized this when he received a telephone call from the President:

> The President called me Monday and asked me to accept the appointment as Alternate on the International Commission for the trial of certain war criminals. (The International Military Tribunal for the Trial of Nazi War Criminals). I talked the matter over with him yesterday and he put the matter up to me as a matter of duty in such a way that I felt there was nothing that I could do but accede to his request. The President assured me that this appointment would have no bearing whatever upon the Supreme Court matter.

Quite obviously, the appointment to the Tribunal in Nuremberg had everything to do with the Supreme Court matter. The President was not going to send Judge Parker to Germany to begin participating in what would be a long drawn-out affair if he had any plans to nominate him to the Supreme Court. Within a few days of Parker's conversation with the President, Senator Hoey wrote to Parker:

> Regardless of the determination of this matter, I think you may feel very happy over the fact that a larger number of senators and congressmen together with judges and citizens at large endorsed you than any other person under consideration; and this applies to the whole country. It is an unusually fine testimonial to your character, ability and distinguished public service.

President Truman did select a Republican for the post, apparently in order to give some bipartisan balance to the Court. But the appointment did not go to Judge Parker, the man recognized even by President Roosevelt as "the outstanding Republican of judicial timer in this country." It went to Senator Harold H. Burton of Ohio, and old friend and associate of the President during his days in the Senate.

There is an irony, and, indeed, it is a sad irony, in Judge Parker's prolonged involvement in the politics of Supreme Court appointments. When he received the nomination in 1930 as a young man of forty-five with a brilliant future ahead of him, the politics of the United States Senate prevented him from taking his seat. After he went on to build a distinguished career as an appellate court judge, and would have been confirmed easily by the Senate at any point over a twenty year period, the politics of the White House prevented another nomination from being made. Such is the importance of time and circumstance in the politics of the American judiciary.

IV

The Bar and The Judiciary

A good lawyer ought to be a good man; and no good man should seek to defeat justice merely because his client will benefit thereby.

The supreme consideration for an appellate court is to keep the law straight.

Judicial independence cannot exist without judicial responsibility.

John J. Parker

One of John J. Parker's colleagues at the bar once described him as "a lawyer to the finger tips." This is certainly a true statement; as a schoolboy in Monroe, an undergraduate and law student in Chapel Hill and as a practicing attorney for fifteen years he was a strong, determined and fairminded advocate of the causes in which he believed. But the statement is also true in a more important sense. Judge Parker believed that the law was the one most essential element in the preservation of democratic government and a democratic way of life. And democracy, in his mind, was the only way of arranging a public order if the liberty and dignity of the individual was to be nourished and preserved.

After fifteen years his interest in the ordinary practice of law began to wane; the mundane necessities of the profession, preparing briefs, arguing cases, filing appeals and advising clients were beginning to wear him down. More importantly, so far as his future was concerned, ordinary practice did not continue to challenge his mind or fulfill his sense of duty. Making money was not one of his goals in life, and he had too much drive to continue doing things that no longer challenged him. Campaigns for elective office had provided an outlet for his energies, but, after his defeat in 1920 and his decision to abandon politics in North Carolina, he turned his mind to new and different things. Parker grew restless in any position that did not allow him to shape the course of events around him. A federal judgeship not only allowed him to do this, it appealed to his sense of duty and brought his mind to bear on matters of public law and government. Not long after he became a judge, he wrote to his brother, "I feel that the public service which I can render on the bench is infinitely more important than the service which I could render at the bar." The appointment to the Fourth Circuit Court of Appeals had come at a propitious time in his career.

Parker's invitation to move to Charlotte in 1922 and to become head of the law firm of Stewart, MacRae and Bobbitt, even though he was a Republican and would be the youngest member of the firm except one, speaks to his standing as an attorney. This move, according to his own explanation, was made for professional reasons, to expand his practice of law. But there was more to it than that; he had reached a turning point in his career and was looking toward opportunities beyond the ordinary practice of law. Although Parker was one of the four leaders of his party in North Carolina, he knew that any future he might have in elective politics in the state was dim. The senior partnership in a prominent law firm in the principal city of the state was a step toward greater opportunities at the national level.

Lawyers And The Bar

Parker had not only grown weary of the routine practice of law, he had become increasingly concerned and displeased with trends developing in the legal profession. He saw a process evolving in which law students were being trained as "clerks," and practicing lawyers were becoming businessmen. The source of the problem, in Parker's view, was in the law schools, especially in the methods of instruction being adopted across the country in the 1920's. Writing to H. W. Chase, President of the University of North Carolina, in 1923 he objected to the planned changes in instructional methods used by the law faculty at Chapel Hill:

... It seems to me that the ideal system of instruction is the lecture system based upon a standard text, with paralled readings of important cases. Of course, no system of legal instruction is worth the name which does not give the student a familiarity with the leading decisions in various branches of the law, but a system which bases its hope of success upon the ability of the average law student to form correct legal conclusions from the reading of reported cases expects too much from human nature. To make a good lawyer under such a system would require not three years, but ten years of study. And after ten years the student would not have as clear a concept of legal principles as a student who had read legal history and studied the writings of eminent lawyers. The case system is essentially an inductive system, whereas the practice of law is essentially a deductive process. The advocates of the case system are talking pure foolishness when they say that legal principles are not sufficiently crystalized to be embodied in a text. As a matter of fact, all legal principles have become crystalized to such an extent that a great percentage of them have been enacted into statutes.

Parker was a Trustee of the University when he wrote this letter. His concern about the changes occurring in the legal profession were real, and he wanted his own institution to be a part of the solution to the problem rather than a party to it. He expressed his displeasure to President Chase about reports that the law professors were no longer requiring students to read the works of Blackstone. He concluded:

> ... I think that the function of the law school is to uphold the ideals of the profession, and that the first ideal of the profession is the ideal of service. The law should be viewed by the student not as a system of geometry or logic, but as an instrumentality through which the life of the people functions. In other words, the law student must be taught not critical thinking, but constructive thinking....

I have quoted this letter to President Chase at some length because it provides a clue to Parker's view of the law and the duty of those who teach the law to prepare students in a certain way. Given the trends in legal education at the time, Parker must have known that he was pleading a lost case. But he was the kind of man who would have his say. He told Chase that the case method was being adopted in universities across the country, not because of merit but

114

because Harvard University was using it. President Chase expressed surprise at Parker's resistance, explaining to him that the case method was being used "in every reputable law school in the country, with the exception of the University of Virginia which sticks to the old method of training." Parker did not have to be told this; he knew it well enough and that is why he was objecting. Law students were being trained as mechanics, not professionals. More and more of them were ignorant of what Parker believed to be the great principles of life upon which all positive law should be based. These new lawyers were using their legal training to gain an advantage in the business world, and were showing little or no commitment to the law as an instrument of public service. The law was being debased and trivialized by the members of the profession itself, especially the law schools.

Parker's criticism of his profession was in a private letter to the President of his own university. But he began to say the same things in public soon after becoming a federal judge and continued to do so until his death. He didn't change his views and he never gave up; he believed one of the greatest threats to the American system of justice would come from lawyers who had never learned or had forgotten that their first obligation was to the public good, not to the attainment of political power or material possessions. Speaking to bar associations, professional conventions and university gatherings over a period of thirty years, he called on the legal fraternity to clean its own house. In a very real sense, he was something of an Old Testament prophet, speaking the same refrain over and over again.

As a federal judge who dealt with lawyers directly in his court, Parker had to be circumspect in his criticisms of the profession. Moreover, despite his sternness, he was a kindly man who treated other people with respect and never resorted to personal attacks or acrimony when matters in which he believed deeply were under dispute. He chose to compliment and persuade rather than scourge those whose behavior he hoped to change. He always prefaced his critical remarks about the legal profession by speaking to the high standards of most members of the bar, and he always said that the lawyers who disgraced the profession were in a small minority. This was a tactic of positive reinforcement; he knew the numbers were larger, otherwise he would not have repeated his fears and criticisms over such a long period of years. But, he saw nothing to be gained by putting down his audiences or placing himself, as a federal judge, in a holier-than-thou position. On occasion his tongue was barbed, because he saw the profession changing for the worse, with a larger percentage of the members of the bar using the law to their advantage and a corresponding decline in the degree of public trust and confidence. Yet, he never resorted to righteous indignation; he appealed to what he believed to be a sense of duty in every man. His criticism of the profession was thus a call for self-reform, a challenge rather than a reprimand. He chose to encourage and lead by example rather than to condemn.

Judge Parker's criticism of the legal profession was, clear and simple, a call to duty, duty to the law as a set of eternal principles and the duty of lawyers to serve the public interest. Lawyers were *officers of the court,* public servants who were charged with serving justice first and clients afterwards. They bore the greatest responsibility for the preservation of moral and ethical standards in public life because they were best equipped, by virtue of their education and experiences in courts of law, to shape the relationships between the private and public sectors. Indeed, Parker believed the shaping of these relationships was the principal business of lawyers. Ministers, teachers and physicians had vital functions to perform among the people, but lawyers were the only professionals who, because of the varied fields in which they worked, could maintain peace and order in society. If they failed in this responsibility, then no other professional group could or would preserve a democratic system based upon a constitution of liberty.

In admonishing lawyers to do their duty, Parker was not only referring to lawyers holding public office, although he assigned to them a special responsibility; he was speaking to the great body of lawyers in private practice. It was these men and women who settled the great majority of disputes and controversies in a society, and it was their duty to settle such conflicts consistent with established principles of justice. The important thing was not the mere settlement of conflict; it was *how* the settlements were reached and the message conveyed to the general public that justice had been served, not just the convenience of the parties concerned. In Parker's views, judges were engaged in the same kind of work. But they were restricted to those controversies that required the application of legal principles through the power and authority of the state. Therefore, the good or evil resulting from the decisions of judges was minor compared to the consequences wrought by lawyers in private practice.

The essence of Judge Parker's complaint was that the legal fraternity was losing its standing as a profession and becoming a skilled trade. He saw three factors contributing to this decline in professionalism; the fact that some lawyers, knowingly and deliberately in pursuit of material gain or political influence, violated the very laws they were honor bound to respect; the fact that an increasing number of lawyers were becoming businessmen who used their knowledge of the law to gain an advantage over laymen; and, thirdly, the growing practice of law by corporations, a development that he believed, perhaps more than all others, contributed to the commercialization of the profession and threatened to debase its commitment to justice and public service. Surely, no one took exception to his first point. But, if the trends in the legal profession since his death are a fair indication, few of his former colleagues at the bar paid much attention to the other two concerns.

Judge Parker called again and again for a code of professional ethics to protect the legal fraternity from its own weaknesses. He wanted legal ethics taught in all law schools, more rigid standards established for admission to the bar and a determined effort on the part of bar associations to purge themselves of those who brought the profession into disrepute. Most importantly, he wanted to see a decided move away from the "sporting theory of the law," the idea of "trial by battle" in which lawyers sacrificed everything in the interest of their client's case and placed winning above all other considerations. It may sound quaint and old-fashioned in our own era, but Parker stated over and over that the purpose of a trial was to obtain the truth, not to win a case for a client. And the legal profession was ill served unless attorneys on both sides of a question viewed a case this way.

Judge Parker was not naive. He knew the world around him was changing and the legal profession was also changing. More lawyers were negotiating business and financial deals than ever before, the practice of law by corporations in the interest of profits not justice was proceeding apace and trial by battle was becoming the norm in the nation's courtroom. In speaking out against such changes and holding fast to a more traditional view of the profession, it might be said by some that Judge Parker was a man behind the times. Perhaps so, but he never stopped trying to persuade the legal profession to his point of view. Another explanation would be that he saw the future more clearly than those around him, recognized the risk of the loss of public confidence in the legal profession and was, as a matter of duty, trying to alert his colleagues to what was happening.

Judges And The Courts

If Judge Parker's ethical and professional standards for lawyers were high, his standards for judges and the courts were even higher. Lawyers and judges were members of the same profession, but with different duties and responsibilities. Where lawyers apply the law in human controversies, judges must declare the law, keep the law straight in all forms of cases and controversies and uphold the Constitution. In regard to the latter function, federal judges in appellate courts (both the circuit courts and the Supreme Court are appellate courts) had, in Parker's view, the inescapable duty of modernizing the Constitution through the reinterpretation of its principles in the light of changing cultural, social and political circumstances. Despite Parker's commitment to stability and certainty in the law he believed that the only way to preserve the principles of law was to assure that precise meaning of these principles did not remain in the hands of those long dead.

In Parker's mind, the law was not a "collection of rules and forms and precedents." It was the "life principle of the organism that we call society —the categorical imperative of organized society, which determines the relationship of the individual to the state and of individuals to each other and prescribes the conduct demanded by the common good." Parker was a working judge; he had to decide cases and apply the laws of Congress and the precedents of the Supreme Court in concrete situations. But he was also a legal philosopher, even though he did not have the time to write about it in the manner of a scholar or professor. Throughout his life he pondered the sources of law and the meaning of law in the affairs of men. Responding to a letter from a clergyman in New Hampshire in 1946 he once wrote:

> I note that you have been reading Pound and Cardozo. Pound is a legal genius, but I agree with you that he is a little wordy. Cardozo was a great lawyer too, but I am not certain that I go along with some of his legal theories. He was a positivist and a so-called realist; and it is hard for me to believe the positivists have ever plumbed the real depths of legal thinking. Law is not something imposed from without, as the positivist like Austin seem to think. It arises out of life; and the more I see of different legal systems the more I believe in the theory of natural law which finds the basis of law in the moral foundations of society. Cardozo and I may be looking at the same things from different angles, but I have always had the feeling that law was more of a mechanical thing for him than it is for me. My approach to the solution of a legal problem is to study the relationships inherent in the situation. I always felt that his approach was primarily to study what legal authority had to say about the matter, which is the positivist approach. With it all, however, Cardozo was a profound philosopher and his positivist philosophy could not blind him to the importance of going to the reason and spirit of the law.

Although there is a vagueness in the concept, Judge Parker believed that the great principles of the law rose up among men out of the general nature of things, out of the fundamental moral foundations upon which human civilizations rested. He often quoted Cicero in discussing the nature of law and would have agreed with the Roman's statement: "I shall seek the root of justice in nature...." But Parker would have argued that law in its most fundamental form came not just from the nature of things but from God, the creator of all things. And in matters of public law and government, it was the peculiar function of appellate judges to keep these great principles alive as they modernized positive law and gave new meaning to the provisions of the Constitution. He believed that a sitting judge, a judge alive and interacting with living people who was aware of existing conditions, needs and modern systems of thought, had greater authority over the Constitution than the "dead hand of the past." The overruling of established constitutional precedents should occur very infrequently and should be done with great care, but no judge worthy of his calling should flinch from this duty if justice so demanded. Parker often quoted Chief Justice Marshall's declaration that the Constitution was "intended to endure for ages to come and consequently to be adapted to the various crises of human affairs." The overruling of prior decisions was one of the most difficult duties of a federal judge. But to Parker it was the proper course to take regardless of adverse public reactions; "When a change of decision of this sort takes place, there are always those who cry that the court is legislating. It is not legislating at all. It is merely applying a constitutional principle to changed conditions."

Parker's insistence on high standards for judges was directly related to his views on the weaknesses and strengths of the federal courts in the political system. He knew that the authority of the courts was essentially moral. The executive had the power of the sword and the Congress the power of the purse, but the courts had only the trust and confidence of the people. The judiciary, more so than the executive and legislature, was the defender of liberty and, if it lost the confidence of the people, it could not preserve liberty and democracy against either political majorities or great concentrations of economic power. Public trust in the courts was tied directly to public trust in judges. For this reason, he never stopped speaking out publicly about the need to maintain high standards in the selection and retention of members of the judiciary.

He had no sympathy for the practice, followed in many states, of electing judges in political campaigns. The sight of a judge campaigning for election and seeking endorsements and support from the lawyers who practiced in his court was repugnant to him. Such practices compromised the independence of the judiciary. He knew most states would never give up this practice so he urged them to adopt the method used in the state of Missouri, a system that provided for the appointment of judges followed by a public referendum after several years to allow the public either to remove them from office or allow them to continue. Since the appointive process was used for staffing the federal courts, Parker's public comments concerned the standards used in the selection process. He called for the appointment of judges of high character, exceptional ability and, most importantly, independence of mind and spirit. By character he meant honesty, courage and an understanding heart; by honesty he meant intellectual honesty as well as complete immunity from any form of financial involvement that would compromise the public trust; by courage he meant the moral fiber to stand alone, if necessary, for what was believed to be right and just. Such expressions, of course, are not unusual. Anyone asked to comment on the standards for federal judges would say very much the same thing. The point about Parker's statements is that he made these remarks again and again all over the country. He was a distinguished judge who was leading an effort to reform the federal courts and improve the administration of justice in the country. In essence, he was saying that procedural reform was important, but in the final analysis, the quality of the judge on the bench was the key to the improvement of justice in the nation.

There is no public office in the American political system as demanding intellectually as the position of an appellate judge, either at the circuit court level or on the Supreme Court. Judge Parker knew this because he lived with these responsibilities every day of his life for thirty-three years. He knew the quality of mind necessary to gaining mastery of the law. He also knew that a federal judge needed a great wealth of wisdom and understanding of the human condition both when declaring the law and applying the law in cases before him. Judge Parker conceded that in some instances legal scholars made good judges, but he preferred candidates who had a great deal of experience at the bar:

> The legal ignoramus has no business upon the bench nor
> ordinarily has the mere legal scholar without practical
> experience in the practice of the profession... the admin-
> istration of justice is an intensely practical matter, and those
> who are to have it in charge should be trained for it through
> practical experience with life and law.

Judge Parker believed that his experience in elective politics served him well as a jurist. It helped him understand the passions and needs of men, their weaknesses and strengths. Politics, as well as the practice of law, brought him into close touch with the ordinary, struggling man in the street. And he came to appreciate how helpless a man could feel when faced with the power of government or high accumulations of wealth and economic power. More importantly, his political experience made him immune to the misconception that the law and the courts stood above politics. Parker knew that the two were inextricably woven together; the courts were integral parts of the political system and appellate judges did not decide guilt or innocence but made fundamental decisions concerning public policy.

No careful student of the federal judiciary can fail to recognize that a court's interpretation of the Constitution "is often the final formulation of national policy." But he also knows that the theory as well as the practice of constitutional government in the United States requires that policy decisions made by courts be proclaimed in constitutional and legal terms. Only in this way can public trust in the system be maintained. In Judge Parker's mind, the trust of the people in their institutions and leaders, especially in their courts and judges, was the *sine qua non* of constitutional democracy. This is the reason he was so single-minded about high moral and ethical standards for lawyers and judges. And it is also the reason he never stopped preaching about the sanctity of law and the Constitution. Certainly some scholars have viewed his public statements on these subjects as simplistic, perhaps even naive. But, he was neither. As a legal scholar working in a very practical world, he knew that the abstruse complexities of a legal and constitutional order had to be translated into terms that were meaningful and acceptable to the people. And the translation had to be from the specific and complex to the general and majestic. Public trust depended upon it. Actually, Judge Parker believed that the most profound truths of life, of law and the Constitution were clear and simple. They were embodied in principles, not in the measurements of behavioral scientists. Therefore, his admonitions to lawyers and judges to do good, to maintain high standards and to cleave to right principles was not only an effort to speak clearly to his profession, it was an accurate statement of what he himself believed.

Parker believed that independence was the most vital quality in a federal judge. He did not just mean independence from the other branches of the government, he meant financial, social, moral, personal and political independence. A judge should have no obligations or connections that would in any way lead people to suspect that justice was not being done in his court. Once appointed to the bench, a judge should put business and political affairs behind him, and should accept no community obligations that had any bearing whatsoever on matters that might come before his court or any other court. A judge should not withdraw from community life, but he should recognize that the constraints on his activities were many and important.

When bad appointments were made or sitting judges proved to be ineffective, incompetent or violated professional ethics, Judge Parker believed that the courts themselves should have the power and means to remove them from office. He called for some form of judicial control; he did not understand, and often said so, why the executive and legislative branches had the authority to clean their own houses but the judiciary did not. The impeachment power was too slow and awkward; furthermore, this power lay in the hands of the legislature not in the judiciary. He called for changes that would allow older judges to retire, but still serve in a part-time capacity. He never called for mandatory retirement, however; and he was adamant and outspoken in his opposition to President Roosevelt's "court packing plan" in the 1930's. He saw Roosevelt's scheme as one of the most dangerous threats to the independence of the federal judiciary in the history of the Republic.

The legitimacy of a political system is often based upon myth, a set of beliefs about leaders and institutions that transcend fact. Such myths become essential to the people's trust in the system, and any weakening of the myth, caused by careful and detailed examination of the life of an institution and publication of findings, can erode public trust and threaten the legitimacy of the system. In this sense, the legitimacy, and therefore the effectiveness, of a system depends upon a truth that is greater than observable fact, a truth that is part myth and part reality. Judge Parker understood fully both the myth and the reality of the federal courts, and he knew that public trust in these institutions rested upon a combination of the two. He knew as much as any man about the imperfections of the judiciary, and the adverse effects of its flaws on the course and substance of justice. Everything was familiar to him: delayed decisions, crowded dockets, inaccurate or non-existent records, inadequate funding, inadequate and poorly paid staff, bad procedures, quarreling judges, badly written opinions, wrongheaded decisions, and bad administrative practices. Parker's repeated appeal for adherence to high standards grew directly from his intimate knowledge of the workings of the federal courts. But he also knew that the authority of the courts was always a tenuous thing, and a muckraking attitude toward them was the very last approach that should be taken by anyone whose ultimate purpose was to improve conditions. Reform and the improvement of the administration of justice were his objectives; therefore he was not only a critic, he was one of America's greatest champions of the federal judiciary. Fully aware of its failings, he never spoke publicly about it in a way that would weaken its influence in public life. His approach was to praise the courts first, and then point out areas where important work was being done to improve them. His sharpest barbs were reserved until after the problems had been solved, and then he would look back and speak directly to how bad conditions use to be, with congratulations extended to those who had helped with the solutions. Judge Parker saw the federal courts as the ultimate bastions of liberty in the United States because of their authority to interpret the Constitution. Throughout his career he repeated this statement: "The enforcement of the Constitution is the most important power and duty of the federal courts, for the judiciary is, in truth, the very keystone of the arch of our Constitutional structure." But he knew that its success and effectiveness in performing this duty rested on the trust of the people, and the trust and confidence of the people was directly tied to the quality of the judges who were appointed to serve them.

District Courts

The federal judiciary is a three-tiered system: district courts, circuit courts of appeal and the Supreme Court. As Chief Judge of the Fourth Circuit Court of Appeals, Parker had direct and personal contact with all three levels of the system. He had the greatest respect and appreciation for the district courts and the judges who served on them. He saw them as courts of great dignity and power, the real "workhorses" of the federal judiciary that bore the heaviest burden of applying federal law and constitutional precedents to the lives of the people. He fully appreciated the problems faced by these courts: daily contact with lawyers, juries and ordinary people in trouble with the law, the ever-present problem of community pressures and local cultural values and the possibility that their decisions would be reversed by the appellate courts.

Judge Parker was unusually sensitive to the feelings of district court judges about being reversed by his court; he often wrote them personal letters when this occurred, urging them not to take overrulings personally but to just accept them as part of the job. When his court had to overrule a district judge, Parker always tried to assign the overruling opinion to the circuit judge who lived in the area of the circuit where the district judge was sitting. He was, however, not always able to do this. In one situation the Fourth Circuit Court had to reverse a district judge six times in one term. Parker assigned two overruling opinions to each of the three circuit judges for the express purpose of avoiding any personal strain between the district judge and the members of his court. Good relations between all the judges in the Fourth Circuit was crucial to the effective and smooth administration of justice in the five state area, and

Parker, who became Acting Chief Judge in 1927 and Chief Judge in 1931, knew this and spent a great deal of time and effort on this problem. Care and kindness in reversals was one technique he used to this end.

Another technique concerned the procedures used when it was necessary for district judges to sit on the Circuit Court to assist with the work load. When Parker joined the Court in 1925, district judges were being ordered to come to Richmond and serve. Some district judges resented this, believing that the Chief Judge had no authority to order them to assist in clearing the docket of the appellate court. Parker's predecessor operated on the principle that the first duty of the district judge was to the circuit court and then to his own. Judge Parker believed the reverse; the duty of a district judge was to his own court, but it was a good practice to sit from time to time with the appellate judges in order to get to know them and to become acquainted with the work of the entire circuit. So, he began using a different approach; he extended personal invitations to the district judges, explaining that such service would give them wider exposure, enhance their reputations and enable them to deal with the law at a higher level. When a new district judge was appointed to the bench, Parker would invite him to come to Richmond as soon as possible in order to make him feel a part of the work of the entire circuit and to broaden his acquaintance and friendship with the circuit judges.

It was sometimes necessary to juggle these invitations and, from time to time, to avoid them completely. Some district judges disliked serving with certain members of the circuit court, especially during Parker's first years on the bench. In these cases, certain district judges would only be invited when the circuit judge in question was away from the court for some purpose. And if a district judge did not fit into the work of the court for some reason, he was usually not invited to sit again. This was sometimes a matter of personality; more often, it was a matter of competence or limited knowledge of the law. Parker also issued few invitations to district judges who could not write opinions consistent with the legal and literary standards Parker insisted on in his court.

A somewhat more sticky problem arose when it became necessary for the Chief Judge to assign a district judge to hear cases in another judicial district. Uneven case loads required this and the Chief Judge, if he wanted the work of the circuit to proceed smoothly, had to shift district judges around. Some district judges did not want to serve outside their districts, and others did not want any assistance regardless of the backlog of their courts or the delay in clearing the docket. Judge Parker handled these situations with kindness and finesse. Writing to one district judge about such a situation, he said:

> Please do not think that I am seeking to interfere in any way with your handling of your district. I know that you have a heavy burden of work and have cheerfully helped out in other districts. You are entitled to assistance under the statute, if you desire it. Whereas the statute, prior to amendment, merely gave me the power to make assignments, the amendment imposes the duty where there is any delay resulting from the accumulation of business.

As a rule, district judges assisting in other districts did not like to hear cases that required the writing of opinions or any other duties once they had returned to their own courts. Parker encouraged a practice that would allow visiting judges to hear only criminal cases and minor civil cases. Cases in equity, patent and bankruptcy cases and other cases that might require later consideration by the sitting judges should be postponed until the resident judge could handle them. Parker knew that local lawyers usually wanted things done this way, so he acceded to this practice.

As Chief Judge, Parker performed what might properly be termed a teaching function. He devoted much attention to improving the performance of district judges. He maintained a close watch on the dockets in every district court, and required reports on all cases remaining on a docket longer than six months. He encouraged district judges to read opinions handed down in other circuits across the nation, and urged them to keep abreast of the manner in which the Supreme Court was handling constitutional issues. This supervision of district courts did not stop with procedural or substantive matters; Parker reacted to the correctness of decisions and the quality of opinions coming from the district courts. Writing to one judge in South Carolina, he once said, "I do not want you to think that I am picking at your opinions; but this is a question of practice which may cause trouble in future cases if we do not get it exactly right." The point of the matter is that Judge Parker viewed any problem in any district court or with any district judge as his own problem. He involved himself privately in the appointment of district judges and in efforts to persuade elderly or ineffective judges to retire. One such effort is instructive; it clearly reveals Parker's firm views on the kind of men who should not be appointed to the federal bench. Writing to a colleague about efforts to gain a district judgeship for a Maryland man, he said:

The more I think of the suggestion made by one of our friends as to filling a possible vacancy in the Maryland courts the more doubtful I am as to the wisdom of his choice. The lawyer that he has in mind is a very able man, but a federal judge ought to be more than an able man. He ought to be a wise man and I am not at all certain that the man he has in mind will meet this requirement. One of the most unsatisfactory federal judges that I have ever known was at the same time one of the ablest lawyers. He knew so much law himself that he would listen to no one else, and was always in a row with the judges of his district. He was reversed more often than any judge of the circuit, and caused endless trouble to the appellate court. When he died the bar of his state breathed a sigh of relief.

Judge Parker's view of the district courts and his relationship with district judges is an important element in his perceptions of the federal judiciary as a whole. He believed that the primary function of the appellate courts, the second tier in the judicial system, was to keep the law straight. He knew that the key to the successful performance of this function by his court was the work of the district courts at the bottom of the tier. His court could not just sit in Richmond reviewing, upholding and reversing district court decisions. The Fourth Circuit had to be viewed by both district and appellate judges as a single entity, with district and appellate judges performing the same functions, the administration of justice, but in different ways. The single most important step toward achieving this goal was the establishment of friendly and cordial relationships among all the judges of the circuit. Although district courts were lower in the judicial hierarchy, they were the most important courts in the system; they were closest to the people, carried the greatest burden of federal cases and played the most crucial role in the administration of justice. District judges were to be treated always as equal colleagues. District courts were not single, separate entities; they were integral parts of a single circuit. Judge Parker began working on the problems of integration as soon as he became Acting Chief Judge in 1927, long before Congress set up procedures that required Senior Circuit Judges to perform a supervisory function throughout their circuits as a matter of law.

The Fourth Circuit Court

In 1927, at the age of 42, with only two years of judicial experiences, Judge Parker had to accept the responsibility for the work of the federal courts in a five-state area. He did not hesitate; indeed, he welcomed the challenge. It provided an outlet for his driving energy, placed him in a position of leadership where he could shape the course of events around him and gave him a degree of national prominence. His success lead to his nomination to the Supreme Court, and his much publicized defeat by the Senate made his name known in judicial and political circles across the nation. Although he did not expect it, the Fourth Circuit Court was to be the focus of his world for the remainder of his life. He became Chief Judge of his circuit in 1931 and eventually was to become the Senior Appellate Court Judge in the nation. He gained national prominence as the leader of the effort to improve the administration of justice in the federal and state courts in the 1930's, as an Alternate Member of the International Military Tribunal in Nuremberg and as judicial advisor and consultant to John J. McCloy, High Commissioner of Germany, on the reconstruction of the German court system. In addition to being a recognized expert on judicial procedure, his opinions figured prominently in four of the most divisive areas of constitutional law in the period during and after the great depression and World War II: the New Deal cases, the flag salute cases, the communist conspiracy cases and the racial segregation cases.

Judge Parker's views on the federal appellate courts, the second tier in the federal court system, are reflected in a very general way in the many speeches he made around the country. But these speeches only touched on the subject; his views on the duties, problems and functions of these courts are found mainly in private letters to his colleagues. How he felt about the judicial process at the appellate level comes out in his correspondence with other judges about the routine, rather mundane workings of his court in specific cases and controversies.

Parker believed that the first duty of the United States Courts of Appeal was to keep the law straight. This duty was of peculiar importance because these tribunals functioned at an intermediate level between the district courts that applied the law directly to the affairs of men and the Supreme Court which had the ultimate authority to declare definitively what the law and the Constitution meant. Since only a very small percentage of federal cases reached the Supreme Court, the circuit courts carried the great weight of declaring the law and keeping it straight throughout the judiciary as a whole. More importantly, it was the circuit courts that, in most instances, posed and shaped the legal and constitutional issues that would move up through the system to be resolved by the Supreme Court. Parker knew that the Supreme court could not function effectively or maintain its moral authority as the final arbiter of public policy disputes if the lower courts did not perform their duties properly. It was his duty as Chief Judge to assure that this did in fact take place in the Fourth Circuit. Parker became a dominant figure in the Fourth Circuit almost from the time of his appointment. He was always a warm friend and colleague, but when it came to the law and the business of the court, he was the Chief Judge.

Judge Parker rarely wrote a dissenting opinion, because it was a rare event for his court to hand down a decision that he thought had been wrongly decided. All opinions were circulated to all members of the court in draft form, even to judges who might not have participated in the hearing of a case. Parker felt responsible for every decision and opinion handed down by his court, and he interjected his views on all cases decided, whether or not he had participated in the case. He always did this kindly, pointing out that it was not his business. He would suggest changes in an opinion, and in some cases call a conference of all judges to discuss the difficulties he was having with the conclusions reached by his colleagues. One incident, selected from many, will show Parker's reluctance to allow a decision to be handed down that he thought was in error. In 1940, in a letter to a colleague, he wrote, "I am afraid that you have reached the wrong result in this case." Six days later he wrote an even stronger appeal for second thoughts:

> You will understand of course that I am not seeking to interfere with your deciding this case in the way that you think it ought to be decided; but I hope that you will give very careful consideration to the holding which you are about to make. I am sure it will come as a distinct surprise to the profession ... I do not wish to appear insistent in this matter, for, of course, it is none of my business. I did not hear the argument and you gentlemen did hear it and the responsibility for the decision is yours and not mine. My only thought is that you go slowly and be sure you are right before you hand down the decision, for I believe it will be subjected to considerable criticism by the profession and the legal publications.

It would not be correct to say that Judge Parker's colleagues on the Fourth Circuit Court deferred to him. Judges Northcutt, Soper, Dobie, Sobeloff and Haynesworth were able and distinguished jurists who made up their own minds. But it would be correct to say that these men believed that a case should be reconsidered carefully if Judge Parker thought it had been wrongly decided. They respected him, not just because he was the Chief Judge, but because of his experience, wide knowledge of the law and procedure, and the thorough and careful study he gave to every matter before him. Furthermore, they knew he merely wanted the right decision to be made for the right reasons. In requesting that a matter be reconsidered, he was really insisting that further discussion was needed because something was wrong. They understood his feelings of responsibility for whatever the court did, and the fact that he may not have heard the arguments and was not a participant in a case, did not change anything.

Decision making in the Fourth Circuit Court during Parker's tenure as Chief Judge followed in general the pattern of other federal appeals courts. The Fourth Circuit Court had only three judges and a larger case load than any other appellate court in the nation during many of the years of Parker's leadership. It held four or five terms a year, as well as special terms for special cases or to clear a crowded docket. Parker felt the court should sit in different cities in the circuit in order to keep in close contact with judges and members of the bar in the five-state area. Therefore, the court convened in Asheville, Charlotte, Charleston and other cities as well as in Richmond. The court heard cases on Monday, Tuesday, Thursday and Friday with Wednesday and Saturday reserved for conferences. The judges were expected to have read all briefs and records prior to hearing open arguments in court. After a case had been heard, the judges made a practice of stepping down from the bench and talking with the attorneys. The purpose was to make all parties feel welcome and at ease in the court and to feel comfortable about future appearances. Although a minor courtesy, Judge Parker felt that the process of justice was well served when the members of the bar and the judges knew each other personally.

In conference the judges attempted first to reach a decision that they believed to be right. The junior member spoke first and voted first; conclusions in conference were always tentative, with final decisions postponed until the pertinent authorities had been studied and draft opinions prepared. No opinions were written while the court remained in session unless an early decision was necessary for some reason. Draft opinions were written after the judges had returned to their homes. If serious divisions occurred among the three judges, they were discussed at length in letters and, if not resolved, then another conference was called or a rehearing scheduled. Minds often changed after conference, and even after draft opinions had been circulated. Parker once wrote to Judge Northcutt and Soper:

> My recollection is that we were right much puzzled about this case in conference, but tentatively reached the conclusion that it should be affirmed. A careful study of it convinces me, however, that we should reverse it. I am unable to distinguish the case in principle from....

The rules followed by the Fourth Circuit Court allowed decisions to be handed down between terms; however, Judge Parker followed the practice of doing this on the first day of a new term of court. But, he would sometimes delay decisions if his colleagues agreed. In one instance involving a case from Virginia, the court agreed to hold up a decision until after an election. In several other situations, the court agreed to delay handing down a decision until public feelings about the case had moderated. And, there were many instances when the judges discussed delaying both decisions and opinions until other circuit courts considering similar issues had ruled, or until the Supreme Court made up its mind on closely related issues that had a bearing on their decisions. Judge Parker's belief that an appellate court should keep the law straight made him more willing to delay handing down an opinion than his colleagues seemed to be.

As Chief Judge, Parker assigned the opinions. He had no patience with the practice, not unknown in the federal judiciary, of assigning opinions as a favor to one judge or another. He discouraged specialization in opinion writing, but he did follow a practice of assigning an opinion to a colleague who was most familiar with the law in a particular area. He also tried to assign opinions to a judge who lived in the area of the circuit from which a case originated. Parker held firm and pronounced views on what should be contained in an opinion and how it should be written. He believed strongly in the use of *per curiam* opinions, short unsigned statements giving the decision of the court with the briefest of explanations. Such opinions should be used in cases where the law was settled, when a detailed account of evidence and reasoning would only confuse the legal principle involved, when a lawyer should be rebuked for bringing a trivial appeal to the court and in cases where the evidence was obscene and revolting. Parker saw no reason to fill the law books with extended discussion of details when such details were not crucial to an explanation of the law upon which the decision rested. He made two exceptions to this practice: He urged the use of the full opinions, even in routine cases, if there was any chance that the Supreme Court would review the case or if there were strong feelings in the country about the outcome.

There were no editorial rules in the Fourth Circuit Court governing the writing of opinions. There may not have been any rules, but there were certainly standards, and these were the expectations of the Chief Judge. As Parker once put it, "the Court does have some standards as to brevity, clarity, etc." Appellate court judges take their opinions seriously. They always view them, especially in important cases, as possible contributions to the literature of the law. They do not need the strong hand of a chief judge to shape and discipline their efforts. But district judges sitting with an appellate court sometimes do because opinion writing is not central to their duties at the district level. An appellate court acts and speaks through its opinions; the quality of these opinions determines whether or not the law is kept straight. This is the reason Judge Parker had such pronounced views on what should go into an opinion and how it should be written. He knew that badly written, wrong-headed and overly personal opinions confused the bar, encouraged unnecessary litigation, weakened the courts as protectors of the Constitution and affected the people's trust in the judicial system.

Parker conceded to any judge his own writing style and he was not one to quibble over minor aberrations in the use of the English language. But he encouraged his colleagues to practice clear and direct expression, to be clear and thorough in their references to authorities and precedent, especially Supreme Court precedents, and to remain sensitive to the general readability of their opinions. He did not like long, wordy opinions full of details. He believed a court of law was just that, a court of law; it was not a school room, a university lecture hall or a debating society. Opinions should explain the law as briefly as possible and should contain no reference to the judge's views about the wisdom of the law or the lack of it. Writing to a colleague about an opinion, he once said:

> I suggest also that the last sentence of the paragraph be changed to something like the following: 'there is nothing that we can do but enforce the law as Congress has written it.' My reason for suggesting this is that the present language indicates that we are blaming Congress. I do not think we should put ourselves in the attitude of criticizing acts of Congress, however much we may possibly disapprove of legislation.

Parker wanted the opinions handed down by his court to be based soundly in the "stream of the law." Decisions should not only be based on precedents, especially Supreme Court rulings, but should reflect knowledge and understanding of decisions being made by other circuit courts in the country. Decisions of other circuit courts should be cited if relevant, but never critically. Reacting to a colleague's opinion in which another circuit court decision was cited he urged that the words "highly technical and legalistic" be deleted: "I would not appreciate another circuit court of appeals referring to one of my opinions in these terms." In order to keep the law straight, he urged his own court to follow the lead of other circuit courts even when it meant a public confession of error:

> The eighth and ninth circuits have unquestionably taken a view contrary to that which we took in our former opinion, and so has the district court in Massachusetts. It seems to me that the thing to do is to decide this case in harmony with their decisions. It is not pleasant to admit that we committed error in our former opinion, but I am persuaded that we were in error and that the only thing to do is to admit it and set it right. I agree with Edmund Burke that no dignity is to be gained from perseverance in error.

Judge Parker did not like a divided court and he did not like dissenting opinions. He spent much time and effort trying to avoid both; they weakened the authority of the court's decisions and encouraged unnecessary litigation. In conference he looked for common ground where all the judges could stand and still do justice to the parties in a case. He was willing to change his own draft opinions, and encouraged his colleagues to do so, if such changes would bring a dissenting judge to the majority position. He felt that dissenting opinions usually did more harm than good; they fostered resentment on the part of the losing party and introduced elements of uncertainty where certainty should prevail. He refused to accept the view, and he was adamant about this, that a judge had a duty to cling to his own views after the majority had determined otherwise. To do so, in Parker's mind, was often nothing more than a guise to make public the debates of the conference room:

> Sometimes a dissent is an appeal to the "brooding spirit of the law." More often it is nothing more than an expression of individual pride of opinion... a judge is taking himself much too seriously if he feels impelled to file a dissenting or concurring opinion everytime his own opinion does not coincide with that of the majority.

In important cases when his court was divided on a constitutional question, and long discussions and rewrites did not resolve the differences, Judge Parker encouraged dissenting opinions. In such circumstances, a dissenting opinion would put the issue squarely before the Supreme Court. This was one of the vital functions of a circuit court, and in such cases a dissenting judge was doing his duty by refusing to go along with the majority. Parker's standards for dissenting opinions were just as rigorous as those he applied to majority opinions: dissenting opinions should discuss the case and the law applicable to it and not the majority opinion. Nothing should be included that might appear offensive to the majority, and the dissenting judge should avoid discussing points that might be of interest to the losing party but were not directly relevant to the grounds upon which the majority decided the case. When a dissent was certain to come, Parker took special care in editing the majority opinion to assure that nothing was said that might offend the dissenter:

> My reason for making this change in my opinion is that if you file a dissent some person might construe the language at present appearing in the opinion as a reflection upon your views, and of course I have no intention of doing anything of the sort.

Three themes run consistently through Judge Parker's views on decision-making in the Fourth Circuit Court of Appeals: the law must be kept straight, the judge's views on questions of right and justice must be reconciled with precedents established in the great stream of American law and personal relationships based on kindness and mutual respect were absolutely essential to the preservation of the dignity of the courts and orderly administration of justice. As Chief Judge it was his duty to try to see that these ends were accomplished both in his own court and in the district courts of the five state-area under his jurisdiction.

The Supreme Court

In one sense Judge Parker's relationship with the Supreme Court was peculiar. He is the only circuit court judge in American history to be rejected by the Senate and then rise to such prominence in the judiciary that his name was put forward by prominent judicial and political figures for every Supreme Court vacancy over a twenty-six year period. He had to endure the frustration of knowing that the Senate would welcome a chance to confirm him to the High Court, but that the politics of the appointment process in the White House was against him. Furthermore, he had to endure the mild but certain embarrassment of having his name urged on the President by well-meaning friends and newspapers when he knew nothing would come of it. Apart from this prolonged speculation about advancement to the Supreme Court, his relationship with the Court and the justices differed little from that of other chief judges of the circuit courts.

Judge Parker saw few distinctions between circuit court judges and Supreme Court Justices; the differences were matters of rank, not of function. Both were appellate judges engaged in the process of declaring the law and interpreting the Constitution. The important difference was that the Supreme Court was the court of last resort, the final arbiter of constitutional and policy disputes. There was never any question in his mind but that the Supreme Court had the final say about the meaning of the Constitution and that the lower courts were bound by its precedents. Also, it was the only national court in the system with jurisdiction over the entire country and the only court that, for all practical purposes, controlled its own docket. But, most importantly, the Supreme Court did not have to worry about any other court in the country overruling its decisions. For this reason, Parker believed the work of his court and other circuit courts was much more difficult because, as intermediate tribunals, they had to reconcile their decisions with each other. They had to bear in mind what the Supreme Court had done in the past, what it was doing at any given point in time and what it might or might not do in the future. Keeping the law straight as cases moved up through the system and precedents flowed down from the Supreme Court was not an easy task for circuit court judges.

What the Supreme Court might do with a case if it chose to review it was an ever present factor in Parker's mind when his court was making a decision. It was not, of course, the controlling factor but it was important. He frequently reminded his colleagues of this contingency. It came into play not only in the substance of a decision, but in the time assigned to hear a case and even in scheduling terms of his court. Writing to Judge Soper in 1937, Parker said:

> The cases arising under the Wagner Act were argued in the Supreme Court yesterday, and we shall probably have a decision from the Supreme Court before we can hold another term of our court. Incidentally, this might be a good reason for not holding a special term and announcing opinions in any of the undecided cases. In other words, if we let things take the usual course the Supreme Court will doubtless decide the question involved in the cases before our next term of court.

This sensitivity to Supreme Court precedents, and speculation about what the Supreme Court might or might not do with a case, was an important factor in the decision-making process in the Fourth Circuit Court during the years of Parker's leadership. When Supreme Court policy was clear and controlling, Parker would assign opinions in his own court to the judge whose views on the Constitution coincided most closely to those expressed in the Supreme Court decisions. He was willing to wait for clarity and direction, but not beyond a reasonable period of time, if this would help avoid confusion in the law and no injustice was done to the parties in a case. Keeping the law straight was an important factor in all of this, but it was not the only factor; Judge Parker did not want to be overruled by the Supreme Court. He did not take reversals personally, and was not prone to brood about them:

> ... but I am not all chagrined by the reversal.... I have glanced over the opinions again, and if I had to decide the case now, I do not see that I would make any substantial changes in them. The questions involved in both cases were close, and I think that our decisions were sound. I say this with all respect for the Supreme Court, for I can readily understand that they might take a different view with regard to the questions in both cases....

Not all circuit judges can remain so detached. On one occasion when the Supreme Court reversed Parker's court three times in one week, Judge Northcutt wrote, "I personally may eventually get over it, but I am sure that I will never be the same." Judge Parker may not have taken reversals personally, but he certainly took them professionally. He saw them as a reflection on his court, especially if there was even the slightest suggestion in the Supreme Court opinion that his court had been careless, ill-informed or negligent about proper procedure. In 1937 when the Supreme Court had remanded one of Parker's cases, suggesting in a *per curiam* opinion that proper procedures had not been followed, he wrote directly to Chief Justice Hughes objecting to the tone and content of the Supreme Court's statement. Given Parker's usual circumspection in all his correspondence, the letter to the Chief Justice can only be described as "barbed." Parker was angry. After expressing his displeasure and pointing out

145

why his court was correct, and that the Supreme Court's rather casual remarks in its opinion were being interpreted as a reflection on his court, Parker concluded:

> We have been reluctant to intrude this matter upon the attention of one engrossed in the solution of many important problems; but we are loath to have it suggested in the permanent official opinions of the Supreme Court that we were unmindful of our grave responsibilities when, at worst, only a technical error was committed. You can readily see that the matter is of grave concern to us.

Chief Justice Hughes answered Parker in a long letter explaining that the Supreme Court's brief opinion did not "constitute [a] reflection upon the complete devotion of the members of your court to the discharge of their judicial function." Parker accepted this explanation but restated his objections. Both he and his colleagues viewed the Supreme Court's opinion as a form of chastisement unnecessarily and unfairly administered. This dispute was over procedure, not substance or constitutional interpretation. Wise men differ over substance, but Judge Parker did not take lightly any suggestion that he did not know what he was doing in matters of judicial procedures. He had no problem when the Supreme Court took exception to his interpretation of the law: "Ordinarily, I am in favor of standing by a decision and letting the Supreme Court reverse us if we are wrong." If the Supreme Court reversed them, Parker and his colleagues took it in stride. If they were upheld, there was always a quiet celebration. Their pleasure was a bit more pointed when the Supreme Court combined cases from several circuit courts in which the same issue was involved, and decided in favor of the interpretation of the law as decided in the Fourth Circuit Court. When this occurred, it was an occasion for congratulations all around.

Judge Parker held the Supreme Court and its members in high regard. As strong-minded and independent in his thinking as he was, he never waivered in his view that the authority of the Supreme Court was final, and that the lower courts were bound to follow its precedents in regard to the law and the Constitution. But, he did not stand in awe of the Supreme Court, and he was often critical of its decisions especially when his decisions were reversed on grounds that he could not accept, or because of ignorance the law which was sometimes the case. His criticisms, however, were never made in public; they were voiced only in conference or private letters to his fellow judges. In this sense, he was certainly no different from most other circuit court judges who find themselves having to enforce constitutional rules they believe to be wrong. Several of Judge Parker's private remarks about the Supreme Court suggest something of the dilemma faced by circuit court judges: "The Supreme Court has certainly messed matters up by their decisions;" "but of course you never can tell what that court is going to do;" "I cannot keep the Supreme Court from making mistakes."

If there is one outstanding characteristic of Judge Parker's relationship with the Supreme Court, it is his fidelity and consistency in following the precedents of the High Court when he believed these precedents were controlling in cases before him. He departed from this cardinal rule in only one instance, the case of *Barnette* v. *West Virginia State Board of Education,* which will be discussed in another chapter. Where Supreme Court precedent was not controlling or there was ambiguity in the Supreme Court's rulings, Parker decided cases according to his own sense of justice and understanding of the Constitution, readily accepting the fact that the Supreme Court would correct him if it believed him to be wrong.

Unless otherwise bound by clear precedents, it was his duty as a circuit judge to administer justice as he saw it. If Supreme Court precedents were clear, then it was his duty to follow them. If established precedents were wrong or outdated, then it was the duty of the Supreme Court to correct its own mistakes. The integrity and effectiveness of the federal judiciary demanded this kind of hierarchal arrangement. The fair and effective administration of justice, which was the duty of all federal judges, depended, in Parker's mind, on the primacy of the Supreme Court decisions over the decisions of lower court judges.

Judicial Administration

Judge Parker was a jurist, an expert in the law. But he was first and foremost a working judge involved in all the internal workings and details of an intermediate appellate court. Had he been confirmed by the Senate in 1930 and taken a seat on the Supreme Court where he would have been free of administrative duties, he would have certainly devoted more of his time and energies to scholarship, to legal philosophy as it pertains to the judicial function. Indeed, those who knew him best in his early days when he was nominated to the Supreme Court, likened him to the great scholars among Supreme Court justices, and expressed confidence that he would take his place among them. But that opportunity did not come, and he turned his mind to problems that were immediate and pressing in the federal judiciary, problems that complicated the performance of his duty. These were not problems of substantive law; they were problems of procedure and administration.

As an acknowledged expert in these areas, Parker was often asked by publishing companies to write books on legal procedure. He always refused because he was too busy working as a judge. But he wrote articles and made speeches on the topic all over the country and devoted a great deal of time to programs and projects designed to improve the administration of justice in the federal and state courts. In his mind, fair procedure and effective administration lay at the core of a just political order. Liberty rested upon order, order upon justice, justice upon the Constitution and the Constitution upon an independent and efficient judiciary that was committed to the protection of the individual against the power of the state. Thus the duty of judges to improve the administration of justice was as vital to the preservation of democracy as their duty to improve the substance of law.

When Parker became a federal judge in 1925, there was very little integration in the federal judiciary. Relationships within the system consisted mainly of higher court review of lower court decisions. The creation of the Conference of Senior Circuit Court Judges in 1922 was a step toward integration, but not much had changed by 1925. In the Fourth Circuit, Chief Judge Edmund Wadill, Jr. had done very little to integrate the work of the courts in the five-state area in order to improve procedures and administration. The district courts were operating as single entities. When Parker became Acting Chief Judge in 1927, he began almost immediately to exert leadership and supervision within the circuit. As his university and political records show so clearly, he tended to take charge of affairs around him; as Chief Judge, he took the position that the work of every district court in the circuit was ultimately his responsibility. The circuit was a single entity, and the administration of justice could not proceed smoothly until all judges in the circuit accepted this point of view. District courts could not continue to function in their own local areas, following their own rules and procedures with only a distant and indirect connection to the appellate court above them. Parker's persistent efforts to improve opinion writing in the district courts, to establish friendly and continuous contacts between district and circuit court judges and his watch-dog attitude toward the dockets and decisions of the district courts were all attempts to improve judicial administration within the Fourth Circuit.

The most significant step taken by Judge Parker to coordinate the work of the Fourth Circuit was the establishment of a judicial conference in 1931. According to Parker, he did this at the suggestion of several of his colleagues. Judicial conferences had been held on an occasional basis in the Sixth and Eighth Circuits and Parker saw these meetings as a method that might serve to unify his own circuit. The first conference, held in Asheville, North Carolina in June, 1931, was so successful that Parker, using his authority as Chief Judge, called one every year thereafter, making it an annual affair. These conferences, which Parker called "schools of jurisprudence," became the model followed by Congress in 1939 when it required by law that all judicial circuits hold annual meetings to discuss their affairs.

After the first conference in 1931, Parker expanded its membership to include not only federal judges but the presidents and five members of the bar associations of the five states, all U. S. attorneys in the circuit, all attorney generals of the five states, representatives of law schools in the circuit and other members of committees of the various bar associations. Judge Parker took these conferences very seriously; their purpose was neither social nor for the general improvement of the law. The purpose was to improve the administration of justice, and all aspects of the conference were to serve that objective. The programs were to be planned carefully and to deal specifically with problems of the administration of the law in both federal and state courts. Prominent judges from across the country, Supreme Court Justices, law school deans and professors, officials of the justice department as well as appellate and district judges from within the Fourth Circuit were invited to speak and read papers. Parker's specific purpose was to integrate the federal courts of the Fourth Circuit; his achievement was, by establishing the first annual judicial conference in the United States, to provide a model that was to be followed throughout the federal judiciary.

Judge Parker's efforts to improve the administration of justice in the federal courts became national in scope through his involvement in the American Bar Association. In 1937-38 he served as Chairman of the Section on Judicial Administration and participated in the drafting of the Administrative Office Act of 1939. This legislation was probably "the most important statute affecting the federal judiciary since the Judicial Act of 1789." In 1940 he served as Chairman of the Special Committee on Improving the Administration of Justice, and in this capacity he was a moving force in the successful effort to establish committees on judicial administration in every state in the Union. He served on a committee, along with the Chief Justice of the Supreme Court, to advise the Director of the newly created Administrative Office of the Federal Courts, and he was chairman of the committee that drafted a bill passed by Congress to provide court reporters in all federal courts. In 1943 the American Bar Association awarded Judge Parker the ABA Medal for Distinguished Service, a much coveted honor awarded in previous years to such men as Charles Evans Hughs, Oliver Wendell Holmes, Roscoe Pound and

Elihu Root. Among those who remember Judge Parker's service on the committees of the American Bar Association or those who heard him speak on the need for judicial reform in the 1930's or even those who have read his many articles on procedure and administration, few would take exception to a remark made in reference to Judge Parker by one of his colleagues after the great reforms of this period had been completed: "No other man on the bench has influenced to such a great extent the improvement of judicial administration."

During Parker's tenure as Chief Judge, the Fourth Circuit Court carried one of the heaviest case loads of any circuit court in the country. Despite the fact that it had only three sitting judges, it was one of the most efficient, if not the most efficient, circuit court in clearing its docket and handing down decisions on time. This kind of efficiency was also true of the district courts in the circuit. In December 1942, Chief Justice Harlan Fiske Stone wrote to Parker:

> I note from a summary of the cases held under advisement for more than thirty days after submission in the district courts, shown by the reports for the first quarter of this fiscal year, that only one of the fifteen district judges in your circuit had any such cases and that one judge had only one such case. I am not surprised, because we are accustomed to the prompt dispatch of the judicial business in the Fourth Circuit. There is no reason why this good work should not be recognized and I take pleasure in extending my congratulations to you and the district judges of your circuit on this excellent record.

The reason for this is clear — Judge Parker's leadership and his concern and persistent attention to efficient administration.

Parker's life-long concern with procedure and administration might lead a casual observer to conclude that he took a narrow and technical view of the law and the judicial function. Nothing could be further from the truth; he was open, liberal and modern in his view of the functions of law and the court's administration of the law. He spent so much time on procedural and administrative reform because this was the area where he saw the greatest need. He once remarked about this point:

> Substantive law very largely reforms itself as the conditions of life change, whereas the adjective law, being the creation of arbitrary rules, is held back by the inertia, the fear of change and the worship of the past which are the curse of all professions.

Legal and judicial procedures were a means to end — justice in the courts. Procedures should be clear, simple and straightforward and technicalities should be reduced to a minimum. Parker had little patience with the practice of resolving cases on the strength of technical rules. And he had no patience at all with the practice of allowing guilty parties to go free and unpunished because of minor technical mistakes in a trial or on appeal.

Judge Parker believed that an independent judiciary was crucial to the preservation of liberty. The regulatory powers of the state were increasing and the influence of concentrated wealth was expanding. The combination of political and economic power was a great threat to individual liberty, the fundamental principle upon which all other democratic values rested. The duty of the federal courts, lawyers and judges was to protect the liberties of the people by assuring that the actions of the government were consistent with the great principles of American democracy embodied in the Constitution. This could not be done unless the administration of justice within the federal courts was improved. To Judge Parker, this was as a matter of professional duty, and his efforts in this area represent his greatest contributions to the American judiciary.

V

The Constitution
and
The New Deal

We must ever remember that freedom lives, not in a written document, but in the minds and hearts of the people.

What I am saying is that there is full power given the federal government under the Constitution to meet any emergency; and that we are not to assume that the Constitution is being abandoned because in extraordinary times extraordinary remedies are adopted.

John J. Parker

Judge Parker's views on the Constitution were clear, direct, and precise. The Constitution existed for the express purpose of protecting the liberties of the people against the power of the state. The Constitution did not consist of words written in stone; it was a statement of fundamental principles—living, organic standards of law to be interpreted by judges of wisdom, learning and strong sense of fair play. The meaning of the Constitution was not to be derived from ideology, philosophy or some esoteric, hair-splitting interpretation of language. The meaning of the great clauses of the Constitution was to come from history, logic and common sense. And those charged with guiding the evolution of the Constitution and applying law to the lives of the people should be experienced, prudent and practical-minded judges, not philosophers, scholars, ideologues, social reformers or antiquarians.

In giving new meaning to the Constitution, federal judges do not function in a vacuum; they do not receive constitutional truths from some higher authority removed from the everyday affairs of men. And the Supreme Court, the ultimate arbiter of disagreements about the Constitution, does not depend solely upon its own wisdom; its decisions are shaped by the arguments and opinions of the lawyers and judges involved in cases at lower jurisdictions. All participants in a case, as it moves through the district and appellate courts, become advisors to the Supreme Court. Judge Parker knew, as all lower federal court judges know, that his interpretations of the Constitution became a part of the corporate body of the law when the Supreme Court upheld his decisions and followed his reasoning in its opinions. But neither Parker nor other appellate judges get much credit for shaping the law because the final decisions are not theirs. In the American judiciary, the Supreme Court gets both the credit and the blame for the great decisions that shape the course of Constitutional law. It is a rare event for a district court or appellate court judge to gain recognition or reputation because of his constitutional decisions. His place within the judicial process simply does not allow it.

Parker as Chief Judge of an appellate court carried heavy administrative duties, and he devoted much of his time off the bench to the improvement of procedures and administration in the federal courts. He rose to national prominence because of his work in these areas, not because of his views on the Constitution. This was a matter of duty to him; he saw the improvement of administration as the greatest need in the federal judiciary. But the element of judging that lay closest to his heart, that most challenged his mind, was constitutional interpretation — the process of rethinking the great clauses of the Constitution and applying the law in a sensible and practical fashion to the changing nature of life. But Judge Parker did not have the forum enjoyed by the Supreme Court Justices, and he did not have time to write books about the Constitution. Therefore, he rarely captured the attention of scholars who write books and articles about constitutional interpretation. Moreover, as Judge Harold Medina once said of him:

> His writings do not have the piquance of style, that pepper and salt and pungent turn of phrase that so helped to spread the fame of Holmes and Cardozo and Learned Hand. No mystery hovered about his pronouncements of the law. He was no Delphic oracle who spoke only to those within the sacred circle. The hallmarks of his style are logic and clarity. No one ever doubted what Judge Parker meant to say.

Judge Parker published many articles in legal journals and made hundreds of speeches all across the country. His articles, however, were almost always manuscripts of his speeches, and with few exceptions, were broad and general in nature. They were written for law students and practicing lawyers, not for "those within the sacred circle." Parker adopted a policy early in his career of refusing to comment publicly on any specific legal or constitutional issue that was before his court or that might come before his court. Thus nothing he ever published or commented on in his speeches dealt with the kind of specific constitutional disputes that capture the attention of scholars, professors or editorial writers. On occasion he would comment on some past court case that had complicated or improved the law, but he refused to discuss publicly any specific constitutional issue that was still controversial. His specific views on the major constitutional issues of his era are to be found only in his private papers and in his decisions buried in the *Federal Reporter*. Although Parker's articles and speeches were very general in nature, they are important because they explain the broad principles that shaped his interpretations of the Constitution in specific cases and controversies.

In Parker's mind the value of the Constitution was instrumental; it was a means toward a greater end — the preservation of democracy in American society. The function of judges was not to preserve the Constitution as a document, but to preserve democratic values and democratic government by wresting the principles of the Constitution from the "dead hands of the past," giving them new meaning in order to meet the needs of living generations. Only by reinterpretation and modernization could these principles be preserved in a society buffeted by cultural, economic, and political change. But the process wherein the Constitution was changed had to be slow and orderly, a historical process that did not respond to greed, drives for special advantage, or the pressures of concentrated political and economic power. The direction of Constitutional change had to rise up out of the lives of the people, its shape and pace determined by the federal courts. And the federal judges were to remain sensitive to historical authenticity and the need to maintain fairness and balance in the public order. Parker believed that sudden and precipitous changes in the Constitution, forced upon the nation by powerful economic blocs or temporary political majorities, were just as destructive of democracy as no changes at all. Political power had to be expressed through law; Judge Parker disapproved strongly of governmental action, however humane its intent, that did not rest upon established law and did not draw its authority from existing constitutional understandings as expressed by the courts.

Democracy was not merely a form of government; it was a way of life. And liberty was the fundamental value from which all other democratic values were derived. But liberty to Judge Parker meant *liberty under law;* restraint was an integral part of the whole system of freedom that the Constitution was established to protect. These two values, liberty and restraint, had to be constantly balanced against each other if a democratic way of life was to endure. Judge Parker did not fear the American people in the exercise of their liberty; he had great faith in them when they were wisely led. He himself was a product of the plain people of North Carolina and no charge or accusation against him stung quite so much as the charges made in the Senate in 1930 by Senators Borah and Norris that he was a reactionary, an enemy of the working people:

> ...Of course, the idea that I ever was a reactionary is pure nonsense. My whole life has been a struggle for freedom and against the forces, social and economic as well as political, which tend to circumscribe a man's life or limit his opportunities. As you know, I had quite a struggle to get started as a boy, and my attitude is one of sympathy for men who are struggling.

Judge Parker did not fear the people when the norms and institutions of society maintained respect for law. But he did fear the powers of government in the absence of restraint. Nothing disturbed him quite so much as the trends, so evident in the world during his tenure on the bench, toward the concentration of political power in governments and the corresponding decline in the importance of personal and social institutions. He was deeply pessimistic about the preservation of democracy in societies where both political power and economic power became concentrated in the same hands, either in the hands of government or particular segments of the population. He did not believe that the liberty of the people could or would survive such combinations. This is the reason he was hostile toward any form of collectivist politics where political and economic power were combined: facism in Italy and Germany, communism in Russia or the various forms of state socialism taking root in Western Europe. Such movements expanded the power of the start to dangerous proportions; they regimented society and circumscribed liberty as to make it practically nonexistent or entirely subject to the whims of those in public office. In Judge Parker's mind any form of totalitarian politics and democratic politics were simply contradictions in terms.

Three principles in the American Constitution were essential to the preservation of a democratic way of life and a democratic form of government: the principle of federalism and the dual sovereignty of the states, the principle of separation of powers, and the Bill of Rights. Judge Parker's commitment to these principles was not rooted in some ideological or philosophical system, but in logic, common sense and historical experience. His fifteen years as a practicing politician at the state level and his vast experience in adjudicating legal and constitutional disputes in court convinced him that the United States was simply too large and diverse to be governed by one national government. Liberty was best served when government was left in the hands of the people and local authorities on matters that concerned them alone. Only matters that concerned the whole people should be the concern of the central government.

Judge Parker's commitment to the principle of separation of powers reflected his fear of concentrated power. Liberty was best protected when the powerful institutions of the federal government possessed the constitutional authority to check each other. Restraint depended upon such an arrangement, especially the authority of the judicial branch to check the elective branches of government. This was the key protection against passion, greed, self-interest and the sway of temporary majorities. The Bill of Rights was the crucial element in Judge Parker's belief in the Constitution as the ultimate protection of the liberties of the people:

> It is easy to believe in freedom of religion for Baptists or Catholics or Presbyterians. The question is, are we willing to accord that freedom to crackpots or infidels or atheists? It is easy enough to believe in freedom of speech for Republicans and Democrats. The test is whether we believe in that freedom for those whose philosophy we hate and consider dangerous and unsound... Unless speech is free for error, it is not free for truth.

Judge Parker never joined that small fraternity of American jurists who believed that the liberties cited in the Bill of Rights were absolute in nature, immune from any restraint from government. In this sense, he remained in the mainstream of American constitutional jurisprudence. Liberty in America was liberty under the law, and the interpretation of its meaning and its application to public affairs was a practical affair. The meaning of liberty was not a matter to be determined by philosophers, political scientists or other word-smiths engaged in a game of semantic analysis. Judges had to do this, and it was their duty to interpret the meaning of liberty in a manner that linked the past, present and future in a continuous and consistent stream of thought. Stability, predictability, and justice had to be so combined as to establish an "ordered scheme of liberty" in a diverse and changing society.

The law had to be kept straight and the Constitution had to be preserved. Both objectives could be achieved, not by abandoning established interpretations under pressure, but by the reinterpretation of the great clauses of the Constitution to make them applicable to changing circumstances. Judge Parker often quoted Chief Justice Marshall's famous words: "We must never forget that it is a Constitution we are expounding... a Constitution intended to endure for ages to come, and consequently, to be adapted to the various crises of human affairs." Parker argued that in modernizing the meaning of the Constitution, the courts were not abandoning its principles; they were, in fact, preserving them. Flexibility was thus a key element in his attitude toward the Constitution. But, it was a flexibility restrained by a commitment to order and stability; a belief that the people's trust in the Constitution and the courts rested, not upon the outcome of each individual case, but upon the gradual adaptation of constitutional principles to circumstances that assured orderly change rather than uncertainty in the law.

Judge Parker believed that "the Constitution belongs to the people, not the government." The people were sovereign, not the government; the Constitution, laws, executive and legislative procedures and administrative rulings were to be interpreted in ways that served the interest of the people, not the government itself. He never lost touch with the common man, and he had greater respect and affection for those he sometimes called "the humble people" than he did for the leaders and power-brokers of American society. His faith in the people, his belief that they had a right to remain free from undue governmental regimentation and allowed to develop themselves, and his belief that they should be protected from oppressive political and economic conditions that lay beyond their control lay at the heart of Judge Parker's concept of constitutional government. This belief is demonstrated clearly in the New Deal cases that came before his court during the 1930's.

The New Deal Cases

The first charge hurled at Judge Parker during the Senate debate of his nomination to the Supreme Court in 1930 was that he was a reactionary, an enemy of the common man, a mouthpiece of big business corporations who would sanction the enslavement of the American working man. As a Southern provincial of limited experience, the charge continued, he had little understanding of the social and economic conditions of the modern era. Within five years of his rejection by the Senate, Parker was referred to in the national press as a "New Deal Judge" who, by expediting cases in his court, was trying to embarrass a reluctant Supreme Court to move ahead and settle the matter of the constitutionality of New Deal legislation. The charge that he was a reactionary was, of course, not true. The reference to him as a New Deal judge was misleading because it was only partially true. Parker had some serious misgivings about some of the legislation passed during the New Deal, but he never questioned the constitutional authority of the Congress to act in an effort to ease the economic plight of the people during a time of crisis.

Judge Parker made his views on this question public in two speeches given before any of the New Deal legislation reached his court or the Supreme Court. The first speech, entitled "Is the Constitution Passing?", was given before the American Bar Association in Grand Rapids, Michigan, in the summer of 1933, and the second, entitled "The Crisis in Constitutional Government," before the Florida State Bar Association in March, 1934. These two speeches, later published in legal journals, spelled out in clear, simple and direct terms why Parker felt that the New Deal, in principle, was consistent with American constitutional principles and traditions. After the first address appeared in print, Thurman W. Arnold, Dean of Yale University Law School, wrote to inform Parker that he had referred the article to government lawyers and urged them to use Parker's reasoning in defending New Deal legislation. He then said to Judge Parker:

> I think everyone connected with the enforcement of the recovery legislation owes you a debt of gratitude for making a clear statement of the case which shows that it is not necessary to tear down the Constitution in order to sustain these acts.

Judge Parker believed that open discussion and free debate were essential to productive change in a democratic society, but he also knew that the line between honest differences that enlivened and improved society and constitutional conflict that threatened fundamental political agreements was thin and tenuous. He was uneasy in 1933 because he saw definite signs of the latter in the controversy surrounding the New Deal recovery programs. The threat to the Constitution came from both wings of the political spectrum: the "ultra-conservatives" who clung to form and assigned "a false sanctity to mere incidentals of our constitutional system and to mere acts of legislation which are by no means essential to the underlying structure," and the "ultra-progressives" who "lose substance in their desire for change of form" and "see in the system nothing but the dead hand of the past which holds man back in his striving for the ideal." Judge Parker saw both groups as extremists. The conservatives were a threat to the constitutional system because "by failing to meet the changing conditions of the world, (they) may wreck the system" they wanted so much to preserve. The progressives were equally dangerous because in "blind enthusiasm for the ideal, (they) may sacrifice the very principles upon which alone the ideal may be measurably attainable."

The fundamental principles of the Constitution were enduring — applicable in all ages under any conditions. The principles must be preserved whatever the time and circumstances, but succeeding generations, especially judges, had the authority, duty and obligation to interpret the meaning of these principles to serve the interest of liberty. Judge Parker rejected categorically the idea that the principles of *laissez faire* economics were bound up with the United States Constitution. And he rejected with equal strength the idea that democracy demanded and the Constitution allowed the state to "take over all productive industry and confiscate private wealth used for productive purposes." Indeed, it was his view that the Constitution was specifically designed to protect the liberties of the people against either alternative. Any philosophy of the Constitution that so restricted the powers of the government that it could not protect liberty was a threat to democracy.

Democracy could only survive "where society (government) controls in social matters and the individual in individual matters." And by confusing the meaning of words and arguing that "all matters are matters of social concern," and therefore subject to public control, "is to make the individual the slave of the state and to crush out his initiative, his energy and his ambition." Freedom and popular government, in Parker's mind, simply could not flourish under either extreme. A sound and balanced interpretation of the Constitution, an enduring concern for constitutional principles rather than form and incidentals, and a value system that placed human liberty over all other values could prevent the nation from abandoning the established traditions that had served it so well.

In these speeches Judge Parker refrained from commenting on any specific issue involved in the legislation before Congress at the time. But to document his conviction that greater regulation by the federal government did not violate the basic constitutional principles, he voiced his support for the Sherman Anti-Trust Act of 1890, the Clayton Act and the acts establishing the Federal Trade Commission and the Interstate Commerce Commission:

> Certainly if Congress may legislate for the purpose of preserving free competition, it may, when this free competition is on the verge of destroying industry itself, legislate to eliminate its destructive features and in the interests of controlled co-operation.

Expanded governmental regulations were necessary to relieve the economic crisis. Government was operating within its constitutional sphere in encouraging agriculture, education, industry and road building. With the nation in the depths of its most severe economic depression and with its people suffering from conditions beyond their control, the federal government, given the impotence of state and local governments when confronted with problems of such magnitude, was the only agency capable of coming to their assistance:

> ...in time of national distress, when the industry of the country is prostrate as a result in large measure of the collapse of interstate commerce and foreign commerce, there is nothing in our Constitutional theory which prevents the national government using its powers for the relief of suffering and to place industry again on its feet.

Judge Parker believed that if the government did not act to relieve the distress of the people, passion and despair would combine to push the nation toward some form of collectivist politics. And in his mind, such a development, whatever its form, would mean the ultimate end of constitutional democracy. In advocating greater governmental regulation, and arguing that expanded regulation was constitutional, he was trying to prevent widespread government regimentation rooted in some ideology that he believed to be alien to the American experience and the spirit of the American people. So he called for greater regulation by the federal government, but he urged caution in both pace and scope. The sovereignty of the states should be respected and every effort should be made to restore their powers and responsibilities toward their own citizens. State and local governments should be assisted in solving their own problems. Only in this way could federalism be preserved. The creation of a huge federal bureaucracy to supervise and regiment American society was the last thing Judge Parker wanted to see develop. He believed that such an institution was in itself a threat to the Constitution because of its low degree of accountability and the conservative and self-serving tendencies inherent in its regulatory functions. The Constitution gave ample power to the federal government to deal with emergencies; under no circumstances should emergencies be used to revamp the entire constitutional structure or to relax established restraints on governmental power.

To the extent that Judge Parker can be said to have had a philosophy of the Constitution, it is embodied in these general observations. His view that the value of the Constitution was instrumental in nature, a document designed to grant power to government but at the same time restrain power was central to his whole approach to public affairs. In working out a balance between liberty and restraint he followed the dictates of his own conscience, common sense and knowledge of history and the law. Professor Horace Williams was correct in his estimate of Judge Parker when he said, "Nobody will succeed in putting a label on you." Judge Morris Soper, Parker's colleague on the Fourth Circuit Court, came close when he described his friend as "a staunch and fundamental constitutionalist" whose mind always remained open to the need to modernize and improve the court's interpretation of the law.

Five of Judge Parker's decisions in New Deal cases show the extent to which the general remarks made in public speeches are reflected in the reasoning in specific cases in law during a period of economic crisis. His first decision was handed down on March 2, 1935, in the case of

Campbell v. *Alleghany.* A federal district judge had ordered
the reorganization of the Alleghany Corporation under the
authority of Section 77B of the Bankruptcy Act of 1934.
The order provided for a scaling down of debts as well as
payments to creditors in some form other than money.
Campbell, a creditor of the bankrupt corporation, claimed
that Section 77B was unconstitutional because it authorized
the seizure of property without due process of law. The
district judge rejected this claim and Campbell appealed to
the Fourth Circuit Court.

During the spring of 1935 the Supreme Court, as
Justice Robert H. Jackson has so aptly put it, "was
hesitating between two worlds," and its policy relative to the
constitutionality of the New Deal was not clearly established.
The previous year in *Home Building and Loan Association*
v. *Blaisdell* and in February, 1935, in the *Gold Clause
Cases* the Supreme Court had shown a sympathetic attitude
toward certain aspects of the recovery program. On the
other hand, in *Panama Refining Co.* v. *Ryan,* decided in
January, 1935, it had struck down as unconstitutional certain
sections of the National Industrial Recovery Act.

Neither the Supreme Court nor any of the appellate
courts, however, had passed on the constitutionality of
Section 77B of the Bankruptcy Act when *Campbell* v.
Allegheny came before Judge Parker for decision. The Act
had been applied, without question as to its constitutionality,
by the Appellate Court of the Tenth Circuit, and the
Appellate Court in the Seventh Circuit had sustained Section
74 of the Act against similar objections. In the absence of a
Supreme Court decision dealing specifically with the
Bankruptcy Act Parker decided the case according to his
own view as to its constitutionality. He said in part:

> Doubts as to the validity of Section 77B are based very largely upon the fact that the relief which it provides for embarrassed corporations, their creditors, and stockholders, has not heretofore existed under the laws of this country, and for that reason seems novel and questionable. It must be remembered, however, that the power granted Congress over the subject of bankruptcy is plenary, and that in its exercise Congress is not limited by what has been attempted in the past but may shape its remedies in a way to meet adequately the problems of the present. Like other constitutional grants of power, that giving Congress power over bankruptcies is to be interpreted, not in the light of conditions with which the framers of the Constitution were familiar, but of what is required under modern conditions.

Quoting at some length from the *Blaisdell* case, Parker dwelled upon the necessity of interpreting the Constitution in the light of existing circumstances. He observed that in order to violate due process the provisions of the Bankruptcy Act would have to be so grossly arbitrary and unreasonable as to be clearly contrary to the fundamental law. Holding that conditions justified such legislation, Parker affirmed the district court decision and upheld the constitutionality of Section 77B of the Act. In so doing he followed, and obviously approved of, the reasoning underlying Chief Justice Hughes' opinion in the *Blaisdell* case.

One month later, in the case of *Bradford* v. *Fahey,* Judge Parker handed down his second opinion dealing with the constitutionality of the New Deal. A district judge had ruled that Section 75 of the Frazier-Lemke Act, designed to give relief to bankrupt farmers, was in violation of the due process clause of the Fifth Amendment. After hearing the case on appeal Parker wrote to the other two judges who sat with him, "I have gone into the constitutional question rather more fully than I intended, but inasmuch as we are the first circuit court of appeals to pass on this question I thought that we ought not to slight it in the opinion."

Before Parker could hand down his opinion, however, the Appellate Courts in the Second and Sixth Circuits, which had been considering the same question, handed down their decisions upholding the constitutionality of Section 75 of the Act. When this occurred Parker held up his own opinion and debated whether or not to delay handing it down until the Supreme Court could review the case from the Sixth Circuit. In view of the definite possibility that the Supreme Court might reverse these lower court decisions Parker was inclined to wait until the Supreme Court's position was clarified. His colleagues differed with him on this point and urged him to hand down the opinion without further delay. With reservations Parker agreed to do so, and after altering one paragraph in order to cite the cases from the other circuits, handed down the opinion.

In the absence of a Supreme Court precedent on the question at issue, Parker decided the case in accordance with his own views as to the Constitutionality of the statute. Quoting from his recent opinion in *Campbell* v. *Alleghany* concerning the plenary power of Congress in bankruptcy matters, Parker dwelled at length on the plight of the American farmer:

> The situation, which still continues in large measure, was that agriculture throughout the United States was prostrate and despairing. A huge volume of debt, estimated at between eight and nine billions of dollars, had been piled up by the farmers in the period of expansion, and this was represented in large part by mortgages on land. As a result of the decline in the prices of agricultural products, the farmers were without means

to pay even the interest on this huge volume of debt, and there was default throughout the country on agricultural mortgages. Foreclosures on an unprecedented scale were imminent; but such foreclosures, while fraught with ruin to the farmer debtors, would not have resulted in payments of the debts, as land had so declined in value that only in rare instances could it be sold for anything like the amount of the debt against it. To have permitted these foreclosures to proceed would have meant the purchasing of land by lienholders, the eviction of owners who were settled on the land and a great increase in tenant farming. It was in the public interest that the farmer be kept on his farm, that, if possible, his interest as an owner of the farm be maintained and that its value as a going concern be preserved.

Parker then quoted the now famous statement by Chief Justice Hughes in the *Blaisdell* case:

While emergency does not create power, emergency may furnish the occasion for the exercise of power. 'Although an emergency may not call into life a power which never lived, nevertheless emergency may afford a reason for the exercise of a living power already enjoyed.' The constitutional question presented in the light of an emergency is whether the power possessed embraces the particular exercise of it in response to particular conditions.

Observing that the Sixth Circuit Court of Appeals had upheld the constitutionality of Section 75 of the Act, Parker rejected the reasoning of the district judge and declared that the Frazier-Lemke Act was constitutional. The following day he wrote to a colleague explaining his decision not to delay handing down the opinion:

As you doubtless saw from the papers we handed down the opinion in the *Frazier-Lemke* case yesterday. I do not know what the Supreme Court is going to do with the case from the sixth circuit, but I felt we ought to go ahead and announce our decision irrespective of the outcome in that case.

On May 27, 1935, a day now recorded in the annals of American Constitutional history as "Black Monday," the Supreme Court handed down three decisions which erased all doubt about its attitude toward the New Deal recovery program. In one of these three cases, *Louisville Bank* v. *Radford* the Court struck down the Frazier-Lemke Act as unconstitutional, thus reversing Parker's decision in *Bradford* v. *Fahey,* as well as the case from the Sixth Circuit which was the case actually before the court for review. Mr. Justice Brandeis, speaking for a unanimous court, declared that action under the law constituted seizure of property without just compensation. The much needed relief for the American farmer, which Parker had so strongly emphasized in his opinion, was thus denied. This case, together with the other two cases decided that day, set the stage for a series of subsequent decisions which threatened to wreck the New Deal.

The effect of these decisions on the implementation of Congressional legislation in the nation was not long in coming. As Justice Robert Jackson so pointedly observed, "hell broke loose in the lower court" with hundreds of injunctions being issued restraining governmental officials from carrying out the will of Congress. Judge Parker was much chagrined by the Supreme Court's decision on the Frazier-Lemke Act but he reluctantly accepted it as law.

The following year in the case of *Wright* v. *Vinton Branch Bank* a district judge in the Fourth Circuit held the

Frazier-Lemke Act unconstitutional on the authority of the *Radford* case. Parker heard the case on appeal but before handing down his opinion wrote to Judges Soper and Northcutt who sat with him in the case:

> It seems to me that it might be wise not to hand down this decision until the Supreme Court acts upon these petitions for certiorari, and if it grants certiorari in any of these cases, to withhold our decision until the Supreme Court acts. Since our experience in the first *Frazier-Lemke* case I have lost my enthusiasm for deciding questions which are pending in the Supreme Court.

Judge Soper, urging Parker to hand down the opinion without delay, pointed out that the opinion reflected distaste for the *Radford* decision and should be changed lest it be taken as criticism of the Supreme Court. Parker responded:

> It was not my intention to criticize the decision of the Supreme Court in the *Radford* case but merely to call attention to the argument based on the *Blaisdell* case and to show that that argument had been fully considered by us and that we thought it was met by the decision in the *Radford* case. I thoroughly agree, however, that we should not use any language which could be construed as a criticism of the Supreme Court and the fact that Judge Soper so construes the language in the latter part of page 6 of the opinion is sufficient grounds for eliminating it.

On October 6, 1936, Judge Parker, knowing that the possibility definitely existed that the Supreme Court would reconsider its decision in the *Radford* case, handed down his opinion in *Wright* v. *Vinton Bank*. Citing the *Radford* case as authority he affirmed the lower court decision and ruled that the Frazier-Lemke Act was unconstitutional.

On February 22, 1936, Parker handed down an opinion in the case of *Greenwood County* v. *Duke Power Company.* Duke Power Company had gone into a federal district court in South Carolina seeking an injunction to prevent Greenwood County from constructing a dam at "Buzzard's Roost" on the Saluda River. Federal funds for this project were made available by the National Industrial Recovery Act. The power company claimed that the sections of this Act which made the funds available for such purposes were unconstitutional. The district judge agreed with the power company, ruled the disputed sections of NIRA unconstitutional, and issued an injunction stopping work on the dam. The county authorities appealed the case to the Fourth Circuit Court.

Parker heard the case but again hesitated to hand down his opinion because of uncertainties surrounding the Supreme Court's attitude toward the government's power programs. He wrote to Judge Soper:

> I have finished the first draft of my opinion in the *Buzzard's Roost* case, but am holding it to hear what the Supreme Court does on Monday before putting it in final shape.

While he waited the Supreme Court handed down its opinion in the case of *Ashwander* v. *Tennessee Valley Authority.* The issues were not the same but the Supreme Court ruled against the power companies. The government thus gained a small victory in its fight to implement its policies in the area of electric power.

The following week, evidently taking his cue from the *Ashwander* decision, Parker handed down his opinion reversing the district court and upholding the constitutionality of the section of NIRA in dispute. Again he dwelled upon the disastrous effects of the depression and held that the enactment of the challenged provision was clearly within the powers of Congress. He saw no Congressional intent to interfere illegally in local concerns. Congress merely established a program of public works to relieve a condition of nationwide unemployment that was threatening the safety, morals, health, and general welfare of the people. Stating that the crisis was jeopardizing the very stability of government, he said in part:

> In light of our history, it is idle to say that, in the presence of such a situation as confronted Congress, the national government must stand by and do nothing for the relief of the general distress, confining its activities to matters as to which it is given legislative powers by the Constitution. It is the only instrumentality which the people of the country have which can deal adequately with an economic crisis nationwide in scope; and there can be no question but that, for the purpose of dealing with such a crisis, it can exercise the power to raise and spend money under Article I, Section 8, Clause 1, of the Constitution.

Parker cited *United States* v. *Butler,* which had struck down the Agricultural Adjustment Act, to show that the power of Congress to authorize expenditures of public money was not limited by the direct grants of legislative power contained in the Constitution. Distinguishing *Panama Refining Company* v. *Ryan* and *Schechter Poultry Corp.* v. *United States,* he held that the Supreme Court's rule governing the delegation of legislative power did not apply in the Greenwood County situation. Congress had laid down the principles to be followed and the making of loans and grants to effect Congressional policy was, in this case, an administrative function. The details of the public works programs were not the concern of Congress. Judge

Northcutt concurred, but Judge Soper did not agree. In a dissenting opinion, he also cited the *Butler* case and argued that legislative powers had been unconstitutionally delegated to the executive branch and that the entire action amounted to an unconstitutional intrusion of federal power into the domain of the states.

When Duke Power Company carried the case to the Supreme Court, most electric power projects in the country were held up pending the outcome. The Supreme Court deliberated five weeks and then in December remanded the case to the district court for retrial. The remand was in the form of a *per curiam* opinion and was based solely on technical grounds. An authoritative decision as to the constitutionality of the government's power policies was overdue, and since the entire program was being held in abeyance pending the outcome of this case, this resort to technicalities by the Supreme Court was not well received in the legal world. Judge Parker was very displeased with the turn of events because he believed matters of such consequences could and should be settled with dispatch. Writing to Judge Northcutt, who had voted with him in the case, he said:

> I note that the Supreme Court has sent the *Buzzard's Roost* case back for retrial. I am sorry that this has occurred for I fear that the impression will be created that the Supreme Court is simply delaying a decision in the matter. I have seen an abstract of the opinion and am not impressed with its strength. All of the facts were fully set forth in the record, and we dealt exhaustively with the merits. It seems to me that it would have been better for the Supreme Court to have passed upon the merits of the case than to have thus delayed the decision in so important a controversy. I feel that at all events we did our duty and that there was no occasion for misunderstanding of our order on the part of the district judge.

In the retrial, Judge J. Lyles Glynn, a close personal friend of Parker's upheld the constitutionality of the section of NIRA in question. Parker wrote to him shortly thereafter, "I see that you have handed down an opinion in the Buzzard's Roost case and I am glad that you have it out of the way. As the matter will probably be appealed to me I shall, of course, express no opinion about the decision." When Duke Power Company filed its appeal Parker scheduled the hearing for a special summer term of the Fourth Circuit Court to be held in Asheville, North Carolina.

In the meantime, the Supreme Court had adjourned, leaving many important cases on its docket and had been criticized for leaving its work undone. Parker's decision to hear the *Buzzard's Roost* case in a special term of the court, so soon after the Supreme Court remand and retrial, was construed in some circles as a deliberate attempt to embarrass the vacationing Supreme Court justices. Columnist Drew Pearson wrote that Parker had "taken another healthy crack at his would-have-been colleagues" by expediting the case and thereby forcing the Supreme Court to decide on the constitutionality of the government's power program without further delay.

Holding a summer term in Asheville was a routine procedure in the Fourth Circuit. Pearson's assertion that the scheduling of the *Buzzard's Roost* case was a deliberate effort of a New Deal judge to embarrass the Supreme Court by drawing national attention to its leisurely summer was, therefore, without foundation. Nevertheless, the extent to which the matter was publicized led Parker to explain his position to the Supreme Court. In letters to Chief Justice Hughes and Justice Roberts he explained the scheduling of the summer term and assured them it was routine procedure. His explanation was accepted graciously by both justices. Although Parker's purpose was not to embarrass, he did in fact schedule the case for an August hearing for the express purpose of expediting the case and getting it back before the Supreme Court during its October term.

Between December 1936 the date of the remand, and August 1937, the date Parker heard the case on appeal for the second time, the Supreme Court executed an abrupt change in its policies and accepted as constitutional all the major postulates underlying the New Deal. The Supreme Court thus resolved the uncertainties in its decisions that had created so much confusion in the lower courts. Citing cases decided during those months as authority, Parker affirmed Judge Glynn's decision and upheld the constitutionality of the NIRA.

In June 1936, Parker handed down an opinion in the Case of *Virginia Ry. Co.* v. *System Federation* upholding the constitutionality of the amended Railway Labor Act of 1934. He noted that the original Act of 1924 had been upheld by the Supreme Court and that the amendment merely established the necessary machinery to implement the will of Congress as embodied in the earlier legislation. In addition, the Act, as amended, required employers to recognize and bargain with employee's representatives and to desist from interfering with lawful efforts of the employers to organize for the purpose of such negotiations. Parker then held that the legislation was a valid regulation of interstate commerce and a reasonable regulation in the aid of collective bargaining. The need for industrial peace was sufficient justification for the establishment of the mediation board. On March 27, 1937, the Supreme Court, largely following the reasoning embodied in Parker's opinion, upheld the constitutionality of the Railway Labor Act as amended. This case became one of the leading cases in the country concerning the enforcement of collective bargaining in labor disputes.

Judge Parker's belief that the Constitution gave ample power to the federal government to cope with the economic crisis of the depression years was tied directly to his commitment to the preservation of liberty, and to the independence of the courts in protecting liberty from undue restraint. The depression and the social despair of the times was a threat to the freedom of the people; a threat that placed in jeopardy the trust of the people in their own government. The great clauses of the Constitution allowed appropriate remedies, but these were remedies to preserve liberty, not expansive schemes to regiment the people once the crisis had passed. Thus the courts, at the same time they were allowing an expansion of the regulatory powers of government, must restrain these powers to assure that only appropriate and constitutional ends were served.

While justifying the expansion of federal power, Judge Parker called for the restoration of the dignity and responsibility of the states. In upholding the constitutionality of expanded congressional action, he was not suggesting that a blank check be given to political majorities to use governmental power to reshape existing governmental structures or American society itself. As power expanded because of new social and economic circumstances, even greater vigilance was necessary to assure that power was not abused. In his mind, the Constitution clearly allowed the exercise of power during emergencies that would not be permissable under normal conditions. But to ignore constitutional restraints in an emergency or to use expanded powers that had been held constitutional because of an emergency, in order to reshape the nation's social and economic systems was, in Judge Parker's mind, a "destructive and revolutionary doctrine."

VI

The Constitution and National Security

Surely, it cannot be that the nation is endangered more by the refusal of school children for religious reasons, to salute the flag than by the advocacy on the part of grown men of doctrines which tend towards the overthrow of the government.

John J. Parker

By the late 1930's the controversy over the constitutional authority of the federal government to regulate the use of property in the general interest of the welfare of the people was essentially settled. The Supreme Court and the lower federal courts entered into what has come to be known as the era of civil liberties. Court decisions made during this era concerning the rights of the people against the powers of government amounted to nothing less than a revolution in American constitutional law. Judge Parker and the Fourth Circuit Court were fully involved in this revolution and their decisions are an important part of its history. Parker's decisions in the flag salute cases and the communist conspiracy cases show how his views on the Bill of Rights as one of the cornerstones of liberty were embodied in resolving two important controversies that came before his court.

The Flag Salute Cases

The flag salute controversy represents the single instance in which Judge Parker refused to follow established Supreme Court precedents and substituted his own view of the Constitution in resolving a dispute before his court. By refusing to adhere to precedent, Parker, as an appellate court judge, deliberately and knowingly, took it upon himself to overrule a decision of the Supreme Court that was controlling in a case involving the question of civil liberty and national security.

The First Amendment to the Constitution states that "Congress shall make no law respecting an establishment of religion or prohibiting the free exercise thereof." According to the doctrine established in 1833 in the case of *Barron* v. *Baltimore* the Bill of Rights was appended to the Constitution to limit only the powers of the federal government. The provision of the First Amendment dealing with freedom of religion, therefore, was not applicable to state action. The Fourteenth Amendment, ratified in 1867, was not interpreted in such a fashion as to prevent the state encroachment on religious freedom until 1925. Thus for one hundred and thirty-five years the federal Constitution offered no protection to citizens whose religious liberties were abridged by state action.

After 1925, when the Supreme Court began its step by step move to incorporate certain sections of the Bill of Rights into the Fourteenth Amendment, the number of cases involving state abridgment of religious freedom on the Supreme Court's docket increased. Though numerous religious groups were involved in these controversies and a variety of issues were in dispute, the problems of a sect known as Jehovah's Witnesses dominated the attention of the Court. This sect presented a host of problems to the Court for solution, but the most troublesome and persistent issue had to do with the refusal of the Witnesses to obey the state laws requiring flag salutes in public school classrooms.

Basing their convictions on Biblical instructions against bowing down to graven images, the Witnesses forbade their children to participate in flag salute ceremonies conducted in the public schools. This stand by the Witnesses brought them squarely into conflict with local customs and state regulations that required school children to salute the flag. Controversy surrounding the issue grew bitter in many of the seventeen states that required the flag salute and ultimately state courts were called upon to resolve the question. The issue was complicated by increased national tensions growing out of the deteriorating international situation. The flag salute became, in the minds of many citizens and not a few state judges, a gesture of loyalty and patriotism essential to the national security. Since the Supreme Court did not face the issue directly before 1940, state judges and lower federal court judges had no authoritative rulings on which to base their decisions. As a consequence, the compulsory flag salute was not interpreted as involving a question of religious freedom.

Before 1935, the Witnesses were unsuccessful in their efforts to escape state regulations that they believed violated their religious freedom. After 1935, when the number of states passing the flag salute statutes increased, the Witnesses turned to the courts for redress of their grievances.* State courts were unsympathetic and the few cases that reached the Supreme Court of the United States were dismissed on grounds that no federal questions were involved. When the lower federal courts began to show some interest in the matter, the chief legal advisors of the sect decided to seek relief in these tribunals.

The first test of the compulsory flag salute in a federal court occurred in Pennsylvania, a state that had expelled more Jehovah's Witnesses than any other state in the Union. Walter Gobitis, a citizen of Minersville, Pennsylvania, would not allow his two children to salute the flag as was the custom in the local public schools. The local school board, after consulting with state authorities, passed a resolution requiring the flag salute and authorizing the school superintendent to take appropriate action against those who refused to participate. The Gobitis children were promptly expelled. Gobitis, with the assistance of the Witnesses' legal staff, brought suit in the federal district courts.

Both the district judge and the circuit judges, who later heard the case on appeal, ruled that the constitutional rights of the Gobitis children had been violated. In reaching this conclusion, these judges ignored the adverse precedents

---

*My discussion of the background of these cases and the circumstances surrounding the case of *Minersville School District* v.*Gobitis* is drawn from David R. Manwaring, *Render Unto Caesar: The Flag-Salute Controversy* (Chicago: The University of Chicago Press, 1962).

previously established in state courts and rejected the "secular regulation" rule* then prevailing in federal court decisions involving questions of religious freedom. The appellate court reached its decision on the basis of the "clear and present danger" test designed years earlier in a free speech case. This was the first occasion in which this test had been applied in a case involving religious freedom. In essence, the appellate judges held that the refusal of school children to salute the flag, when their religious convictions demanded the contrary, did not constitute a "clear and present danger" to the nation that could be restricted constitutionally.

Aware that the Supreme Court had held previously that no federal question was involved in such controversies, the school authorities petitioned for a writ of certiorari on grounds that the flag salute requirement was constitutional and that the lower court decisions were contrary to the Supreme Court's own precedents. On four previous occasions the Supreme Court had refused to review the state court decisions on flag salute questions. Each case had been dismissed with a *per curiam* opinion on grounds that religious liberty was not involved. The petition was granted, and in view of existing precedents, it was probable that the same fate awaited the *Gobitis* case. The circumstances surrounding this case, however were different. The earlier cases were appealed from state court decisions upholding compulsory flag salutes. The *Gobitis* case came up from the lower federal courts where the judges, disregarding Supreme

---

* This rule holds that religious groups are not excused from obeying state regulations which are designed to control secular activities and are not directed at religion, even though the effect of the regulations on religious activity is considered to be adverse.

Court policy, had ruled that a federal question was at issue and that the religious freedom of the Witnesses had been abridged.

The composition of the Supreme Court and the views of the Justices on the flag salute question are important factors in understanding Judge Parker's role in this controversy after the *Gobitis* case was decided. Chief Justice Charles Evans Hughes dominated the Court during these years and was on record, in the *per curiam* opinions mentioned above, as a firm advocate of the "secular regulation" rule. Associate Justices Owen Roberts and James C. McReynolds had joined Hughes in these decisions; Harlan Fiske Stone, the other pre-Roosevelt member of the Court, had also concurred but was known to have grown more sympathetic toward the plight of the Jehovah's Witnesses. The five Justices appointed by Roosevelt were relatively new to the flag salute question and their views on the subject were not firmly established in 1940. Justices Hugo Black, Stanley Reed, and Felix Frankfurter had participated in some or all of the earlier cases but William O. Douglas and Frank Murphy were facing the issue for the first time.

Hughes, who exerted much influence on the Court, delivered the opening statement in conference, strongly urging that the lower court decision be reversed. Apparently, none of the other eight Justices took issue with his position or expressed any opinion about the issues at stake. The subject was closed with the Court seemingly unanimous in its decision not to affirm. Justice Frankfurter, who was later to become the Court's leading spokesman for the doctrine of "judicial restraint," was assigned to write the opinion. When Frankfurter circulated his opinion for criticism, Justice Stone refused to initial his approval. He later filed a vigorous dissenting opinion strongly objecting to the decision of the majority.

Frankfurter's opinion began with a statement concerning the grave responsibilities of the Court when attempting to reconcile the conflicting claims of liberty of conscience and the interest of the nation. His opinion then proceeded along the lines of the Court's previous allegiance to the "secular regulation" rule. In his mind, the right of the state to require the flag salute in the public schools was beyond question. The point at issue was whether "the requirement of participation in such a ceremony, exacted from a child who refuses upon sincere religious grounds, infringes without due process of law the liberty guaranteed by the Fourteenth Amendment." Restating the "secular regulation" rule in answer to that question, Frankfurter said in part:

> The religious liberty which the constitution protects has never excluded legislation of general scope not directed against doctrinal loyalties of particular sects. Judicial nullification of legislation cannot be justified by attributing to the framers of the Bill of Rights views for which there is no historic warrant. Conscientious scruples have not, in the course of the long struggle for religious toleration, relieved the individual from obedience to a general law not aimed at the promotion or restriction of religious beliefs. The mere possession of religious convictions which contradict the relevant concerns of a political society does not relieve the citizen from discharge of political responsibilities.

Frankfurter then justified required compliance with the rule as a patriotic exercise conducive to national health and unity:

> The ultimate foundation of a free society is the binding tie of cohesive sentiment. Such a sentiment is fostered by all those agencies of the mind and spirit which may serve to gather up the traditions of a people, transmit them from generation to generation, and thereby create that continuity of a

treasured common life which constitutes a civilization. 'We live by symbols.' The flag is a symbol of our national unity, transcending all internal differences, however large, within the framework of the constitution... the precise issue, then, for us to decide, is whether the legislation of the various states and the authorities in a thousand counties and school districts of this country are barred from determining the appropriateness of various means to evoke that unifying sentiment without which there can ultimately be no liberties, civil or religious. To stigmatize legislative judgment in providing for this universal gesture of respect for the symbol of our national life in the setting of the common school as a lawless inroad on that freedom of conscience which the Constitution protects, would amount to no less than the pronouncement of pedagogical and psychological dogma in a field where courts possess no marked and certainly no controlling competence. The influences which help toward a common feeling for the common country are manifold. Some may seem harsh and others no doubt are foolish. Surely, however, the end is legitimate. And the effective means for its attainment are still so uncertain and so unauthenticated by science as to preclude us from putting the widely prevalent belief in flag saluting beyond the pale of legislative power.

The *Gobitis* decision and the reasoning of Frankfurter's opinion represented what appeared to be a fatal setback for the Jehovah's Witnesses. The Supreme Court's decision, by virtue of an authoritative eight to one majority, had been established on this vital question of individual liberty. The concurrences of the five liberal justices appointed by Roosevelt in this decision sustaining the "secular regulation" rule returned the matter to the hands of local and state authorities. The lone dissent by Justice Stone, however, represented a glimmer of hope. It was a strong and pervasive objection to the views of the majority that the effects of the regulation were of secondary importance if its objectives were non-religious in nature. Stone's dissenting opinion was to become an important factor in Judge Parker's involvement in the flag salute cases.

Justice Stone, who was soon to succeed Hughes as Chief Justice, had concurred in the earlier *per curiam* opinions dismissing appeals from the state courts. Though a moderately conservative Republican, he was in sympathy with the liberal position of the New Deal Court on questions involving rights of individuals. In his *Gobitis* dissent, Stone rested his objections squarely on the First Amendment:

> The law which is thus sustained is unique in the history of Anglo-American legislation. It does more than suppress freedom of speech and more than prohibit the free exercise of religion, which concededly are forbidden by the First Amendment and are violations of the liberty of the Fourteenth. For by this law the state seeks to coerce these children to express a sentiment which, as they interpret it, they do not entertain, and which violates their deepest religious convictions.

Conceding that government must be able to act in order to achieve its legitimate ends and that loyalty, patriotism, and national unity were certainly legitimate objectives, he argued:

> So here, even if we believe that such compulsions will contribute to national unity, there are other ways to teach loyalty and patriotism which are the sources of national unity, than by compelling the pupil to affirm that which he does not believe and by commanding a form of affirmance which violates his religious convictions. Without recourse to such compulsion the state is free to compel attendance at school and require teaching by instruction and study of all in our history and in the structure and organization of our government, including the guarantees of civil liberty which tend to inspire patriotism and love of country. I cannot say that government

here is deprived of any interest or functions which it is entitled to maintain at the expense of the protection of civil liberties by requiring it to resort to the alternatives which do not coerce and affirmation of belief.

Stone rejected Frankfurter's views on judicial restraint and forcefully argued that the Court should not refrain from passing on the judgment of the legislature in situations where constitutional rights had been abridged, even though the "remedial channels of the democratic process remain open and unobstructed." To do so, he thought, was to leave the liberty of small minorities vulnerable, protected only by the good will of the majority. The following portion of the opinion reveals clearly Stone's strong convictions on the guarantees which the Constitution provides for liberties of the individual:

> The guaranties of the civil liberty are but guaranties of freedom of the human mind and spirit and of reasonable freedom and opportunity to express them. They presuppose the right of the individual to hold such opinions as he will and to give them reasonable free expression, and his freedom, and that of the state as well, to teach and persuade others by the communication of ideas. The very essence of the liberty which they guarantee is the freedom of the individual from compulsion as to what he shall think and what he shall say, at least where the compulsion is to bear false witness to his religion. If these guaranties are to have meaning they must, I think, be deemed to withhold from the state any authority, to compel belief or the expression of it where that expression violates religious conviction, whatever may be the legislative view of the desirability of such compulsion.

Though the Witnesses had suffered a substantial defeat, the decision used to strike them down soon weakened to the point that the chief legal strategist of the Jehovah's

Witnesses regained some hope of obtaining a more favorable reaction in the federal courts. In August 1942, the legal counsel for the Witnesses filed a bill of complaint in the name of Walter Barnette in the United States District Court, Southern District of West Virginia. Thus began the second stage of the flag salutes dispute in the federal courts, and it was at this stage that Judge Parker became involved.

The bill of complaint asked for a permanent injunction against a resolution of the West Virginia Board of Education requiring the flag salute in that state's public schools. This was a class action designed to obtain relief for all children of Jehovah's Witnesses similarly situated. More significantly, the bill of complaint was the beginning step of a deliberate effort to get the matter before the Supreme Court for reconsideration. In the face of the *Gobitis* precedent, the Witnesses again claimed that compulsory flag salutes constituted a denial of freedom of speech, freedom of religion, parental rights, and was a denial of liberty without due process of law. Lawyers for the state filed a motion to dismiss, claiming the whole matter had been settled by the Supreme Court in its *Gobitis* decision.

As required by law, District Judge Ben Moore established a panel of three federal judges to hear the case. He asked District Judge Harry E. Watkins and Judge Elliott Northcutt of the Fourth Circuit Court of Appeals to sit with him in the case. Judge Northcutt, who had taken a qualified retirement from the bench some years before, still heard cases when his health permitted. According to the rules of the Fourth Circuit he was the appropriate appellate judge to handle this three-judge tribunal because he was a resident of West Virginia. Northcutt became ill and was unable to sit; therefore, Judge Moore telephoned Parker, the Chief Circuit Judge, and asked him to preside over the court. In a letter to District Judge W. Calvin Chesnut, Parker wrote:

> I am planning to go out to West Virginia to sit on a three-judge court next Tuesday involving some sort of controversy about Jehovah's Witnesses in the state of West Virginia. Judge Northcutt was to preside in the case, but Judge Moore has just telephoned me that Judge Northcutt is ill and has asked me to preside.

This was the first flag salute case to come before a federal court in the Fourth Circuit and apparently Parker was not aware of its nature before he arrived in Charleston. Jehovah's Witnesses had appeared in the Fourth Circuit Court on numerous occasions prior to this date but under different circumstances. Usually these cases involved refusals by individual Witnesses to report for induction into the military service and the Court dealt with them in *per curiam* opinions.

We do not know Parker's predisposition toward the issues underlying the flag salute controversy; however, several of his public addresses contain clues to his thinking on the relationship existing between individuals and the government in time of crisis. Parker was an active participant in church affairs and a strong advocate of the idea that religious principles were essential to the health and character of the nation's life. He believed that the Constitution embodied the great principles of the Christian faith, expressed in political terms, and he frequently spoke of "righteousness" as one of the essential ingredients of a just legal system.

Parker was clearly in sympathy with the trend in judicial decisions during this period that provided broader federal protection for rights of the individual. Speaking to an audience gathered for the dedication of a new law building at the University of Louisville in 1939, he said:

When we established our government here and looked to the people and not to a king as the source of power, we guaranteed these fundamental rights to the individual not merely against the power of the executive but against the entire power of the state, so that no public official, no legislative assembly, no popular majority might deny them to any individual, however poor, or humble, or unpopular he might be. This, I think, was America's greatest contribution to the science of government. Without it, the rights of the individual would be subject to the whim of majorities and the tyranny of the demagogue, and democracy would perish here just as it perished in Athens and in all the democracies of old. With us power is derived from the people and popular majorities represent the people's will; but we recognize that government must represent justice and righteousness as well as power; and we will not permit the power of the state to be used to do injustice to the individual — to deprive him of those fundamental rights which belong to him as a man.

Parker was also a strong patriot: he fully approved of the objectives of World War II and was highly critical of domestic controversies that tended to distract the nation from its international problems. Appealing for national unity before the Federal Bar Association of the District of Columbia in 1942, Parker discussed the problems of a free and democratic society when faced with an external threat to its security:

No selfish interest, no racial prejudice, no class objection must be allowed to stand in the way of all-out unified effort. There is entirely too much dissension and discussion in our ranks. Napoleon once said, 'Wars have been won by good generals; wars have been won by bad generals; but no war has ever yet been won by a debating society.' We cannot all lead; we have chosen our leaders. They must determine for us the policies to be followed in the prosecution of the war. And we must give them unified support. They will make some mistakes, of course, but the mistakes will soon be corrected and will amount to little if behind them is the loyal support of a united people. Of course, free speech and the right of petition must be preserved, but here policies have been decided upon and the time for action has come, we must not hamper action by continuing to debate or by attempting to reverse the decisions of our leaders by stirring up public discontent.

In this appeal for an end to internal dissension and prolonged debate on policies already determined, Parker was not advocating compromise of the people's liberties. He rejected completely the argument that the Bill of Rights could be suspended in emergencies. In his view, freedom of thought, of speech, freedom of conscience, and the right not to be deprived of life, liberty, or property without due process of law, "were the rights of free men in war as well as in peace."

On the same day that Judge Moore acted to set up the three-judge panel, legal counsel for the Jehovah's Witnesses filed a second motion asking for an interlocutory injunction against the school board until the case came up for trial. In the hearing called to consider this motion Judge Parker was "openly critical"* of the whole affair. He urged the state authorities to excuse the children of Jehovah's Witnesses from flag salute ceremonies. He then recessed the hearing to give the state authorities time to consider his request. The hearing was reconvened the next day, and when informed that his suggestion had been rejected, "Parker received word of the Board's intransigence with open disgust, commenting that it was 'unfortunate that a case of its kind should be in

---

* My discussion of Parker's conduct and remarks during the hearing are drawn from Manwaring's excellent account of these incidents.

court at a time when national unity is paramount.'" Parker then rejected the state's motion for dismissal on grounds of the *Gobitis* precedent, "curtly remarking that dismissal on that ground will not easily dispose of this case." Neither party disputed the facts in the case so a trial seemed unnecessary. Opposing counsels agreed to the issuance of a final decree based on the briefs and on the pleadings which had just been made in the hearing on the motion for an interlocutory injunction.

In conference, Judge Parker and the two district judges agreed that the resolution of the State Board of Education making the flag salute compulsory in public school classrooms was a violation of the First and Fourteenth Amendments to the Constitution. As was the custom in the Fourth Circuit, conclusions reached in conference were only tentative. Final decisions were delayed until all members of the court had returned home and reviewed carefully the pertinent authorities. On September 21, Parker, who had decided to write the opinion himself, wrote the following lines to Judge Watkins:

> I have been thinking about the case that we heard, and the more I think about it the more firmly I become convinced that our tentative decision was correct. I shall get up the opinion promptly when the pleadings are all in and submit it for your consideration.

On October 3, Parker sent his finished opinion to Watkins and Moore for their review and criticism. He also sent a separate statement of his findings of fact, conclusions of law, as well as copies of the Supreme Court's briefs in the *Gobitis* case. Parker's correspondence does not reveal whether or not the two district judges made any criticisms or suggested any changes in the opinion. On October 6,

Barnette v. *West Virginia State Board of Education* was handed down, declaring that the compulsory flag salute in public school classrooms was a denial of religious freedom, and therefore a violation of the First and Fourteenth Amendments to the Constitution. This decision was squarely opposed to and in direct conflict with the precedent the Supreme Court established two years before in the *Gobitis* case. This was the first time in seventeen years on the bench that Parker knowingly and deliberately refused to follow a clearly established Supreme Court ruling in a case involving a constitutional issue.

Normally, in cases where the point at issue was close or where the judges were unhappy with Supreme Court precedents governing a question, they wrote to each other concerning their doubts, suggesting alternate decisions, and discussing possible consequences resulting from any decision agreed upon. Frequently they speculated as to how the Supreme Court would react to their decisions. No correspondence of this nature seems to have taken place concerning this case. Apparently, the three judges were of one mind on the question or the two district judges chose not to take issue with the Chief Judge's decision. Any discussion they may have had about the risks or the propriety, in disregarding the *Gobitis* precedent occurred in conference and thus is not a matter of public record. Explanation for the decision, therefore, must be found solely in the opinion.

After briefly stating the facts in the case, Parker introduced his opinion in a fashion which, to that date, was unique in his judicial experience. He explained why he was not going to follow the law on this subject as established by the Supreme Court:

Ordinarily we would feel constrained to follow an unreversed decision of the Supreme Court of the United States, whether we agree with it or not. It is true that decisions are but evidences of the law and not the law itself; but the decisions of the Supreme Court must be accepted by the lower courts as binding upon them if any orderly administration of justice is to be attained. The developments with respect to the Gobitis case, however, are such that we do not feel that it is incumbent upon us to accept it as binding authority. Of the seven justices now members of the Supreme Court who participated in that decision, four have given public expression to the view that it is unsound, the present Chief Justice in his dissenting opinion rendered therein and three other justices in a special dissenting opinion in *Jones* v. *City of Opelika*, ... The majority of the court in *Jones* v. *City of Opelika*, moreover, thought it worthwhile to distinguish the decision in the Gobitis case, instead of relying upon it as supporting authority. Under such circumstances and believing as we do, that the flag salute here required is violative of religious liberty when required of persons holding the religious views of plaintiffs, we feel that we would be recreant in our duty as judges, if through blind following of a decision which the Supreme Court itself has thus impaired as an authority, we should deny protection to rights which we regard as among the most sacred of those protected by constitutional guaranties.

Judge Parker was obviously in agreement with Stone's dissent rather than the position of the majority in the *Gobitis* case, as expressed by Frankfurter. In the case of *Jones* v. *Opelika,* referred to above, the Supreme Court in a five-four decision had ruled that a non-discriminatory tax levied by a town government on the sale of religious literature by Jehovah's Witnesses was not a violation of religious freedom. In a dissenting opinion in that case Justices Black, Douglas, and Murphy not only objected to the majority position but added that they were of the opinion that the

Gobitis case had been "wrongly decided." Further, Chief Justice Hughes and Justice McReynolds, both of whom had voted to sustain the flag salute in the *Gobitis* case, had been replaced on the court by Robert Jackson and Wiley Rutledge. Thus, of the eight-judge majority in the *Gobitis* case, only Frankfurter, Reed, and Roberts remained on record as approving the decision. Apparently Parker engaged in a bit of "nose counting" and concluded that the authority of the *Gobitis* precedent had been substantially undermined.

Though neither his opinion nor his correspondence suggest that Parker took judicial notice of the after-effects of the *Gobitis* decision, he was certainly not unaware of them. The *Gobitis* decision was contrary to the general trend of the Supreme Court's decisions in civil liberty cases and was unpopular in many quarters. School expulsions had increased, persecution of Jehovah's Witnesses had intensified, and apparently as a result of the negative reaction to the decision, numerous state courts had refused to be bound by it.

Judge Parker pointed out in his opinion that there was nothing improper in a state requiring the flag salute and that he personally approved of such ceremonies because they encouraged a love of country. Also he saw nothing in the flag salute that reasonably could be held in violation of Biblical commandments or any other duties man might owe to his Maker. But, he continued, the views of the court as to the reasonableness of the requirement were irrelevant. Plaintiff's objections to the salute were based on religious scruples and it was their views, not those of the court, which were involved in the question. To force them to salute the flag under such circumstances or to deny them rights and privileges as citizens because they refuse to salute was, in his mind, to deny them the religious freedom guaranteed by the Constitution.

As to the duties of a citizen, and the rights of the state to restrict liberties in the interest of the public weal, Parker listed the various practices which the courts had refused to sanction even though rights of religious freedom were involved. He then expressed himself as to whether the compulsory flag salute belonged on that list:

> To justify the overriding of religious scruples, however, there must be a clear justification therefore in the necessities of national or community life. Like the right of free speech, it is not to be overborne by the police power, unless its exercise presents a clear and present danger to the community ... Religious freedom is no less sacred or important to the future of the Republic than freedom of speech; and if speech tending to the overthrow of the government but not constituting a clear and present danger may not be forbidden because of the guaranty of free speech, it is difficult to see how it can be held that conscientious scruples against giving flag salute must give way to an educational policy having only indirect relation, at most, to the public safety. Surely, it cannot be that the nation is endangered more by the refusal of school children, for religious reasons, to salute the flag than by the advocacy on the part of grown men of doctrines which tend towards the overthrow of the government.

Parker then posed the question directly. "Must the religious freedom of plaintiffs give way because there is a clear and present danger to the state if these school children do not salute the flag as they are required to do?" To ask such a question was to answer it in the negative. The flag salute was, in his mind, a fine ceremony, but only indirectly related to the national security. The abstinance of a few school children involved no danger to the state.

Parker's reliance on the "clear and present danger" test followed closely the usage of Judge Clark of the Third Circuit Court in his decision in the *Gobitis* case. Parker's elaboration on Clark's reasoning, and his handling of the question in this case, marks the most complete and forceful use of the "clear and present danger" test in cases involving religious liberties. It was the sole basis for his decision as no reference was made to the "secular regulation" rule which Judges Maris and Clark had distinguished, and which Frankfurter had relied on completely in the *Gobitis* decisions.

Consistent with his strongly held view that the federal courts formed the "arch of the constitutional structure," Parker curtly dismissed Frankfurter's appeal for judicial restraint. Such restraint, he argued, nullified constitutional guaranties of freedom of religion and left the people vulnerable to the state's police power, the extent of which would be merely a matter of legislative discretion. "For the courts to so hold would be for them to abdicate the most important duty which rests with them under the Constitution." Throughout his judicial career Parker had preached the doctrine of limited government based on a written constitution; thus, he was completely in character in saying:

> ... the tyranny of majorities over the rights of individuals or helpless minorities has always been recognized as one of the great dangers of popular government. The fathers sought to guard against this danger by writing into the Constitution a bill of rights guaranteeing to every individual certain fundamental liberties, of which he might not be deprived by any exercise whatever of governmental power. This bill of

rights is not a mere guide for the exercise of legislative discretion. It is a part of the fundamental law of the land, and is to be enforced as such by the courts. If legislation or regulations of boards conflict with it, they must give way; for the fundamental law is of superior obligation.

Parker's concluding statement is something of a peroration; it reveals his strong feeling on matters of human conscience and explains his own personal views of the responsibilities of American judges. Declaring that coerced flag salutes were void under the Constitution, he said:

> The salute of the flag is an expression of the homage of the soul. To force it upon one who has conscientious scruples against giving it, is petty tyranny unworthy of the spirit of this Republic and forbidden, we think, by the fundamental law. This court will not countenance such tyranny but will use the power at its command to see that rights guaranteed by the fundamental law are respected.

The reaction to Judge Parker's dismissal of the *Gobitis* precedent was mixed. The Chairman of the Board and the General Counsel of the American Civil Liberties Union wrote that they were "particularly gratified at the vindication of the principle of religious liberty which your decision so eloquently voices." Those who were inclined to be concerned about the "means" used by judges in arriving at decisions, however, were less pleased with Parker's treatment of the Supreme Court precedents. Appellate Judge Calvery Magruder of the First Circuit Court of Appeals, writing at a later date in the *Cornell Law Quarterly,* expressed strong doubts about the propriety of Parker's departure from the policies of the Supreme Court. After recounting his own experience of following a never-overruled precedent of the Supreme Court and then being reversed for doing so, he said:

On the other hand, it appears to me that the three-judge court in the fourth circuit, in the second flag salute case, did an unseemly thing in counting noses, so as to speculate as to whether the Supreme Court, as reconstructed, would be likely to adhere to its ruling in the first flag salute case, decided only a few years earlier. It was no less unseemly, though in the result Judge Parker guessed right as to what the Supreme Court would ultimately do. Statistics will show that in these two cases the Court of Appeals for the First Circuit got itself reversed whereas the Fourth Circuit got affirmed. But that only goes to show that statistics do not necessarily tell the full story.

In view of the discrepancy between Parker's decision and the established precedents, it was a foregone conclusion that the *Barnette* case would be reviewed by the Supreme Court. When the state's appeal was granted, Parker indicated to the American Civil Liberties Union that he was very pleased that the Supreme Court was going to reconsider its previous position on the flag salute question.

In June, 1943, the Supreme Court in a six to three decision affirmed Judge Parker's decision, specifically overruling the *Gobitis* precedent and the earlier *per curiam* opinions. Justice Robert Jackson, who wrote the opinion for the majority, did not base his decision on the First Amendment as Parker had done but concluded, in short, that no constitutional authority existed for a state to require anybody to salute the flag. The details of his opinion need not be considered here; however, it is appropriate to consider briefly the long and strongly worded dissenting opinion filed by Justice Frankfurter. Obviously piqued by Jackson's point by point rebuttal of his *Gobitis* opinion and Parker's effrontery in disregarding it as authoritative, Frankfurter again defended his stand on the flag salute. He literally denounced the use of the "clear and present danger" test which had been the principle basis for Parker's decision and had been alluded to by Jackson:

> To apply such a test is for the court to assume, however unwittingly, a legislative responsibility that does not belong to it. To talk about 'clear and present danger' as the touchstone of allowable educational policy by the states whenever school curricula may impinge upon the boundaries of individual conscience, is to take a felicitous phrase out of context of the particular situation where it arose and for which it was adopted.... He [Justice Holmes in *Schenck v. United States* in 1919] was not enunciating a formal rule that there can be no restriction upon speech and, still less, no compulsion where conscience balks, unless imminent danger would thereby be wrought 'to our institutions or our government.'

In earlier cases, speeches, and in personal and official correspondence, Judge Parker said repeatedly that lower courts judges must follow Supreme Court policy regardless of personal preferences and that any other course of action would lead to chaos in the federal judiciary. He prefaced his opinion in the *Barnette* case with this same admonition, and then proceeded to do exactly the contrary. It is inconceivable that Parker would have advocated such a policy as a general rule to be followed by lower court judges. It is also likely that he would have frowned upon lower court judges engaging in "nose counting" and anticipating what the Supreme Court would be likely to do in the future rather than what it had done in the past. Except for this one case, his past record clearly reflects a belief that it was the business of the Supreme Court to overrule its own precedents. Parker's resort to "nose counting" in the *Barnette* case was, to say the least, unusual. This second guessing of the Supreme Court was not characteristic of his decision-making and was, in effect, a deliberate attempt to justify his departure from the law as declared by the Supreme Court. Such an explanation would have been unnecessary for a Supreme Court justice who could simply have observed that the existing precedent was based upon an erroneous interpretation of the Constitution. As an appellate court judge, however, Parker had no such freedom in reaching his conclusions. In spite of his sense of justice and his obvious belief that the law had been wrongly decided in the *Gobitis* case, he was forced, because of his own convictions concerning the proper role of an inferior federal judge, to engage in this process of rationalization to escape that embarrassing precedent.

Parker's decision, however, if viewed in a different light, is characteristic. On more than a few occasions he had declared that a judge's first responsibility was to administer justice. Judges were not to adhere blindly to outdated precedents established in other times under different conditions. The law, in order to be just, must grow and change with the times, adjusting itself to contemporary circumstances. Furthermore, Parker believed that the most fundamental principle in the Constitution was the preservation of liberty against the coercive power of the state. In the *Barnette* case he had to choose between adherence to a recently established precedent of the Supreme Court, which he believed rested on an unsound and wrong-headed interpretation of the Constitution, and his own sense of justice and constitutionality. He chose the latter.

The Communist Conspiracy Cases

Judge Parker was an unabashed patriot; he never minced his words in praising the American people and the

American system of government. He sincerely believed that the system of constitutional liberties worked out over the years in the United States was the best hope of mankind everywhere. Although he supported movements toward some form of world government based on a system of international law that could be enforced, and praised such organizations as the United Nations and the World Court, he believed that American military strength should remain such that no nation anywhere would ever dare challenge it. He made many speeches calling for a world organization based on law, and knew full well that such a move was the only way to assure a lasting peace. But Judge Parker was not naive about such matters; and with the onset of the Cold War in the 1950's, he spoke frequently about the need for democratic nations to defend themselves against the menace of totalitarian movements. But his speeches in the 1950's were not his first warnings. As a young politician seeking elective office in North Carolina, he warned against the attractions of socialism in societies where social and economic reforms were neglected and the well-being of the common man ignored. In the 1930's, with the nation in the grip of its worst depression and the rise of facism and communism in Europe, he again voiced his fears of collectivist politics and the fusion of political and economic power in the hands of the state. He included socialism on his list because of its tendencies, even in democratic socialistic movements, to abuse the language and define traditional private concerns as social problems and therefore subject to governmental regulation. His views on this subject would not be well received in many quarters today, but he simply believed that liberty could not long flourish in a society where all aspects of social and economic life were subject to governmental regulation. Free government had to rest upon a harmonious community, a community that evolves out of the private and social lives of the people through non-governmental institutions. Community could not be created and maintained through administrative regulations.

Judge Parker's experience as an alternate member of the International Military Tribunal in Nuremberg intensified his fear of totalitarianism, and his residence in Germany as an advisor to John J. McCloy, High Commissioner for Germany, allowed him to see first hand the misery of a great people who had failed to protect their nation against their own internal enemies. These experiences convinced him that a democracy must defend itself. The American Constitution clearly provided sufficient authority for the government to take legal action against its own citizens who actively and knowingly sought to destroy and overthrow a duly constituted and freely elected government. Free government, in Parker's mind, rested on two fundamental principles, reason and force. "Force without reason is tyranny, but reason without force is anarchy." Democratic government, because it must by its very nature remain committed to the preservation of a wide range of freedom, demanded a clear-headed understanding of the tensions between those liberties it must not abridge and those liberties that must be restrained. But those restraints that proved to be necessary had to be consistent with the standards of due process of law as established by the courts.

Judge Parker decided two important cases involving the constitutionality of federal legislation designed to restrict the activities of members of the Communist party in their efforts to bring about the overthrow of the government by illegal means. On July 31, 1952, Judge Parker handed down an opinion in the case of *Frankfeld* v. *United States* sustaining a district court's conviction of several members of the Communist party and upholding the constitutionality of the Smith Act. Parker's reasoning was based squarely on the Supreme Court's decision in *Dennis* v. *United States,* decided the previous year:

> The question presented is not one as to freedom of speech or as to the right to organize for political purposes, but goes to the power of government to outlaw and punish conspiracies whose purpose it is to overthrow the government itself by force and violence. Modern history is replete with instances of the danger to government inherent in such conspiracies; and there is nothing in the Constitution or in any sound political theory which forbids it to take effective action against that danger. If it may take action to protect itself from being overthrown by force and violence, it necessarily follows that it may forbid conspiracies having that end in view and may punish such conspiracies as criminal.

In *Dennis* v. *United States* the Supreme Court, in essence, had altered the old "clear and present danger" doctrine of the *Schenck* case to read "clear and probable danger." In so doing it expanded the legal powers of the government to act against threats to the national security and reduced that area in which individuals could operate free of official restraint. In this case Parker applied the "clear and probable danger" test directly to the activities of the indicted Communist:

> In the absence of conspiracy the 'clear and present' danger rule may furnish a satisfactory criterion of criminality in the case of ordinary speeches advocating force and violence; but such rule has no practical application to advocacy of violence in connection with conspiracies to overthrow the government, for the danger of such conspiracies is ever 'clear and present.' They are pregnant with potential evil, which, while hidden

from view in normal times, is likely to assert itself as an irresistable force when some national crisis presents an opportunity for a putsch or a coup d'etat.

Appellees argued that the membership provisions of the Smith Act were invalid, even though the Act in its entirety was constitutional. Again relying on Chief Justice Vinson's opinion in the *Dennis* case, Parker pointed out that membership is condemned only where there is knowledge on the part of the accused party members of the illegal objectives of the organization. By joining the party, he explained, a person renders aid and encouragement to the organization. And where a person accepts or retains membership in full knowledge of the unlawful purposes of the party, that person becomes a party to the criminal designs of the organization. Obviously in full approval of the means and ends of the Smith Act, and convinced of its constitutionality, Parker concluded:

> Certainly it is within the power of Congress to forbid the circulation of literature advertising the forceable overthrow or destruction of the government or membership in an organization having such destruction as its purpose, where there is knowledge of such purposes on the part of one accepting or retaining such membership.

Three years after his Frankfeld decision Parker handed down an opinion in the now celebrated case of *Scales* v. *United States.* Junius Scales, while a student at the University of North Carolina had participated in Communist affairs as Chairman of the Party in North and South Carolina. As a result of these activities he had been convicted in a federal district court for violation of Section 2 of the Smith Act. This section of the Act makes it a crime to obtain or retain membership in any organization advocating the overthrow of the government by force and violence if the member is aware of the criminal purposes of the organization. In the district court Scales argued that this provision of the Act was unconstitutional. The district judge held to the contrary and the case came before Parker on appeal.

Viewing the evidence presented as essentially the same as that presented in *Dennis* and *Frankfeld,* Parker affirmed the lower court decision and held that the membership provision of the Smith Act, under which Scales stood convicted, was constitutionally valid. Since the principle issue here was membership in the party rather than conspiracy as had been the case in *Dennis* and *Frankfeld,* Scales argued that those cases should be distinguished and that the membership provision was clearly unconstitutional. Parker responded to this reasoning by quoting at length from his *Frankfeld* opinion, and from the opinions of Chief Justice Vinson and Justice Jackson in the *Dennis* case. A conspiracy was a partnership in crime and all who join it with knowledge of its purposes are equally guilty. Membership *per se,* he explained, was not criminal according to the statute. Informed membership, however, means participation in the conspiracy and the constitutionality of legislation designed to cope with such dangers was beyond doubt.

Finally, Scales argued that Section 4 of the Subversive Activities Control Act of 1950 had repealed the membership provision of the Smith Act. This provision, which required members of the Communist party to register with the government, provided that neither the holding of office nor membership in any Communist organization by any person should constitute *per se* a violation of any criminal statute. Judge Parker rejected Scales' argument, pointing out again that membership in the party with knowledge of its criminal objectives was more than membership *per se*. One was constitutional, the other clearly criminal. This interpretation of the effect of the Subversive Control Act on the membership provisions of the Smith Act was Parker's own personal appraisal of the situation because the Supreme Court had not ruled on the question. In 1961 Mr. Justice Harlan, speaking for a 5 to 4 majority of the Supreme Court, sustained Parker's decision and upheld the constitutionality of the membership clause of the Smith Act.

Thus, Junius Scales, a young and impressionable political activist, became the first and only American citizen to be imprisoned for membership in the Communist party. Scales and Judge Parker, the federal jurist who declared his conviction to be constitutional, were natives and residents of the same state and had received their undergraduate education in the same university. Scales, scion of a wealthy and prominent family, gained his view of the world of politics in one era and wanted to reform American society through the application of a political ideology alien to the mainstream of American thought at the time. Judge Parker, son of a working class family, gained his view of politics and law in an earlier era and saw the world from a different perspective. Communism was a form of collectivist politics that represented the antithesis of democracy. Judge Parker believed, and so held in his decision, that the Constitution gave wide latitude to the government in its efforts to restrain the liberties of those who knowingly and actively organized to overthrow public authority by illegal means.

VII

The Constitution
and
Racial Segregation

All men must have equal rights under the law; all men, without regard to race or religion or color and any other circumstances.

It is infinitely better that reform be delayed for a few years than that we surrender the safeguards against tyranny which are contained in the right of the Court to enforce the great general clauses of the Constitution.

Judge J. Parker

The most controversial issue to come before Judge Parker's court during the era of civil liberties was the issue of racial segregation. Race had been an important element in Parker's public career from its beginning. In three campaigns for elective office in North Carolina he was accused of trying to turn the state over to "Negro control." The Senate rejection of his nomination to the Supreme Court in 1930 was due in part to charges that he was a Southern racist who was insensitive to the needs of black people, and his failure to receive another nomination to the Supreme Court during the twenty years that followed the controversy of 1930, was due to some extent to political sensitivities related to the growing influence of the NAACP in public affairs. And the racial overtones in the confusion in the 1950's over the distinction between government sponsored segregation and government sponsored integration led to such a distorted view of Parker as a man and judge that public references to him in some quarters amounted to defamation of character. As late as the mid-1960's, years after his death, *Newsweek Magazine,* echoing charges of an earlier day and apparently without even the most cursory review of public records, referred to Judge Parker as a troglodyte.

Although such charges were unfortunate, they are not surprising given the heated atmosphere of the times. Parker was a Southerner with deep roots in the culture of the South, and he held to a constitutional philosophy that linked public order and peace to gradual social and cultural change rather than passionate political movements endorsed by judicial decrees. As Chief Judge of the Fourth Circuit Court he was responsible for the administration of justice in the federal courts in five Southern states. But, as an appellate judge he could not make definite decisions; where precedents of the Supreme Court were clear and controlling he was duty bound to follow them. Where such precedents were unclear or ambiguous, it was his duty to decide cases according to his own views of the Constitution. It was not possible for Parker, or any other Southern federal judge, to face the issue of racial segregation head-on in court without being subjected to hostile criticism from some quarter regardless of the nature of his decisions.

The Early Segregation Cases

One of Judge Parker's earliest decisions concerning the constitutionality of racial segregation came in the case of *City of Richmond* v. *Deans* in 1930. A Virginia law passed in 1924 "to preserve racial integrity" prohibited blacks from renting or purchasing homes in white neighborhoods. Citing Supreme Court cases as precedents, Judge Parker held that the Virginia law was discriminatory under the Fourteenth Amendment and therefore unconstitutional. Ten years later in 1940, Judge Parker decided the case of *Alston* v. *School Board of the City of Norfolk* and struck down as unconstitutional a Virginia law that discriminated against black school teachers on the basis of race. Melvin O. Alston, a black school teacher in Norfolk, had brought suit on behalf of himself and other black teachers claiming that a state law which established lower salary scales for blacks was unconstitutional. He asked for a declaratory judgement that unequal salaries for teachers of equal qualifications and experience who were performing the same duties was in violation of the due process and equal protection of the laws clause of the Fourteenth Amendment. The district judge dismissed the case on a technicality and the matter came before the Fourth Circuit Court of Appeals.

Parker noted in his opinion that the state of Virginia operated a segregated school system but since the appellants had not challenged this arrangement or made any mention of it at all, no consideration was given to its constitutionality. Two principle issues were before the court: (1) was the fixing of two different salary scales a violation of the Fourteenth Amendment? and (2) if the state law was discriminatory, were any rights actually infringed upon? Speaking to the first issue, Parker pointed out that the city schools of Norfolk were operated according to state law, that teachers were qualified and paid in accordance with state law, and that salaries for school teachers were drawn from public funds raised by general taxation. Clearly, therefore, the action of the city of Norfolk was state action and subject to the restrictions of the Fourteenth Amendment. Declaring that the distinction in the pay scales was obviously based entirely on race, he said:

> That an unconstitutional discrimination is set forth in these paragraphs hardly admits of argument. The allegation is that the state, in paying for public services of the same kind and character to men and women equally qualified according to standards which the state itself prescribes, arbitrarily pays less to Negroes than to white persons. This is as clear a discrimination on the grounds of race as could well be imagined and falls squarely within the inhibitions of both due process and equal protection clauses of the Fourteenth Amendment.

In response to the second issue Parker pointed out that even though the black school teachers were trained professionals, that fact alone did not give them a right to teaching contracts in the public schools. Employment was a matter resting within the discretion of school authorities. But, he added, where they apply for work and are employed, they are entitled to salaries appropriated for the position they fill which have been determined free of unconstitutional discrimination based on race. Parker concluded that Alston, and other blacks similarly situated, were qualified school teachers and had a civil right, as such, to pursue their professions without being subjected to discriminatory legislation on account of race or color. No controlling precedents existed on this subject because the Supreme Court had not decided a case dealing with unequal pay for black school teachers. Parker mentioned one district court decision which had held such salary scales unconstitutional, and then cited a long series of Supreme Court decisions striking down discriminatory state laws. His decision was clearly consistent with evolving policies of the Supreme Court toward state action that discriminated against racial groups. In effect, Parker simply extended an evolving doctrine of the Supreme Court to a different body of facts and, in so doing, adhered to the spirit of the law. The Supreme Court indicated its approval of his decision by denying a petition for a writ of certiorari.

After the *Alston* decision was handed down the state of North Carolina, without further legal action, moved to equalize salaries of black teachers in its school system. Commenting of this development one editor remarked, "the equalization of teacher's salaries in North Carolina and wherever it is occurring in the South is due to the decisions and influence of this great jurist and humanitarian."

Another important constitutional case involving the rights of blacks decided by Parker before the highly publicized controversy of the 1950's was *Rice* v. *Elmore,* handed down on December 30, 1947. The issue involved was the infamous "white primary" used by the Democratic Party in the South to prevent blacks from exercising the suffrage. In a series of cases beginning in the 1920's the Supreme Court struck down as unconstitutional state laws and party regulations that prevented from participating in party primaries. The Supreme Court's action against the white primaries culminated in the landmark case of *Smith* v. *Allwright* decided in 1944. In this case the Court held that party policy denying blacks the right to participate in the nomination of candidates constituted state action and was, therefore, unconstitutional. Blacks thus had a constitutionally protected right not to be barred from party primaries either by official or unofficial state policy.

On April 14, 1944, immediately after *Smith* v. *Allwright* was handed down, Governor Olin D. Johnston of South Carolina called an extraordinary session of the state legislature for the express purpose of repealing all state laws governing primary elections. His objective was to sever any legal relationship existing between the state government and the Democratic primaries. Johnston proceeded on the assumption that state silence on the subject, and the absence of any state laws governing nominations, would provide sufficient grounds whereby the situation in South Carolina would be distinguished from the one just declared unconstitutional in *Smith* v. *Allwright*. It was, in short, an effort to strengthen the argument that a political party was a private organization.

Governor Johnston delivered an impassioned address to the legislators concluding that, "White supremacy will be maintained in our primaries. Let the chips fall where they may." The General Assembly then proceeded to expunge from the state statutes one hundred and fifty laws regulating party primaries. A constitutional amendment was then proposed that would delete any reference to primary elections from the state's fundamental law. This amendment was approved by the people of the state in the next general election. The Democratic State Convention then adopted a new set of resolutions to govern the operation of its primaries. These new rules were virtually identical to the expunged statutes except that the word "election" was omitted. Thus the Democratic party of South Carolina conducted "primaries" or "nominating primaries" rather than primary elections. Whether or not this new arrangement would legally circumvent the Fourteenth Amendment was a question to be decided by the federal courts.

Soon thereafter a black man, George Elmore, brought a class suit in the District Court of the Eastern District of South Carolina. The bill of complaint sought an injunction against officials of the Democratic party to prevent further denial of the right of blacks to vote in primary elections. District Judge J. Waties Waring of Charleston, after hearing the case, ruled the barring of blacks from the primary was in violation of the Fourteenth Amendment. He based his decision squarely on *Smith* v. *Allwright,* which he refused to distinguish. Noting that South Carolina was the only state in the Union conducting a primary election solely for white people, he declared, "It is time for South Carolina to rejoin the Union. It is time to fall in step with the other states and to adopt the American way of conducting elections." The case was appealed to the Fourth Circuit Court of Appeals in Richmond.

Judge Parker, speaking for a unanimous court, affirmed Judge Waring's decision. Following closely the reasoning in Waring's opinion, he elaborated on the constitutional significance of the election practices at issue in the case. After restating the facts, Parker pointed out that the Democratic party controlled absolutely the choice of elective officers in the state of South Carolina because the general election served only to ratify and give legal validity to the party's candidates. And though state party officials had gone to great length to sever the bonds between state and party, in effect, nothing had changed. The Democratic party, following its new procedures, conducted its primary in the same fashion as it had previously done under state law, and the primary continued to served exactly the same function as before.

Appellants attempted to convince the court that the party in South Carolina was a private organization much like a country club and, therefore, had complete discretion in deciding who participated in its activities. Parker rejected this argument. He held that a political party was not a mere association of individuals and the party primary was something more than a piece of party machinery. Primaries, he continued, had become imbedded in the election machinery of the country and the parties which conduct them had become, in effect, state institutions and governmental agencies through which sovereign power is exercised by the people. Parker cited the stream of voting rights cases in which the Supreme Court had declared that state authority was involved in the white primaries conducted by the Democratic party in Texas. Parker then turned to appellants' argument that the situation in South Carolina was not the same:

> It is true, as defendants point out, that the primary involved in Smith v. Allwright was conducted under the provisions of state law and not merely under party rules, as is the case here, but we do not think this a controlling distinction. State law relating to the general election gives effect to what is done in the primary and makes it just as much a part of the election machinery of the state by which the people choose their officers as if it were regulated by law as formerly. Elections in South Carolina remain a two-step process, whether the party primary be accounted a preliminary of the general election or the general election be regarded as giving effect to what is done in the primary; and those who control the Democratic party as well as the state government

cannot by placing the first of the steps under officials of the party rather than of the state, absolve such officials from the limitations which the federal Constitution imposes. When these officials participate in what is part of the state's election machinery, they are election officers of the state *de facto*, if not *de jure*, and as such must observe the limitations of the Constitution. Having undertaken to perform an important function relating to the exercise of sovereignty by the people, they may not violate the fundamental principles laid down by the Constitution for its exercise. We know of no reason why the state cannot create separate agencies to carry on its work in this manner, and when it does so, they become subject to the constitutional restraints imposed upon the state itself.

Parker concluded with a statement concerning the constitutional right of black citizens to participation in the political life of the community. This conclusion reveals Parker's commitment to the principle of equal protection of the laws and well illustrates the evolution of American Constitutional Law in the direction of expanded federal protection for the rights of black citizens:

An essential feature of our form of government is the right of the citizen to participate in the governmental process. The political philosophy of the Declaration of Independence is that governments derive their just powers from the consent of the governed; and the right to a voice in the selection of officers of government on the part of all citizens is important, not only as a means of insuring that government shall have the strength of popular support, but also as a means of securing to the individual citizen proper consideration of his rights by those in power. The disfranchised can never speak with the same force as those who are able to vote. The Fourteenth and Fifteenth Amendments were written into the Constitution to insure to the Negro, who had recently been liberated from slavery, the equal protection of the laws and the right to full participation in the process of government. These amendments have had the effect of creating a federal basis of citizenship and of protecting the rights of individuals and minorities from many abuses of governmental power which were not contemplated at the time. Their primary purpose must not be lost sight of, however; and no election machinery can be upheld if its purpose or effect is to deny to the Negro, on account of his race or color, any effective voice in the government of his country or the state or community wherein he lives. The denial to the Negro of the right to participate in the primary denies him all effective voice in the government of his country. There can be no question that such denial amounts to a denial of the Constitutional rights of the Negro; and we think it equally clear those who participate in the denial are exercising state power to that end, since the primary is used in connection with the general election in the selection of state officers.

Judge Morris Soper, who sat in the case, and heartily concurred in the decision, wrote to Parker that his was an outstanding opinion which the Supreme Court "might well adopt as its own." Judge Armistead Dobie, the third judge in the case, wrote to Parker, "Once more I want to express the view that I am confident this opinion will stand up in the Supreme Court, and I believe it will attract no little attention around these United States."

This case was not "on all fours" with *Smith* v. *Allwright* because no state laws were involved in the South Carolina situation. On the face of things, the *Allwright* case was not directly controlling and, had Parker taken a highly technical view of the matter, he could have found grounds to distinguish the two cases. He refused to do so, preferring to give first consideration to the effect on black voters of the state's non-policy on primary elections. Viewed in this light, the effects were the same, only the schemes to disfranchise were different. Parker's reasoning here was much the same as it had been in the *Alston* case: he extended an existing doctrine to cover different set of facts, and reached a decision clearly consistent with the spirit of Supreme Court rulings in closely related areas of the law. Judge Parker's interpretation of this issue became a part of the Constitution in April, 1948 when the Supreme Court declined to review the case.

By 1948 a full scale attack on the legality of segregation in American society was underway. Under the leadership of the NAACP, black citizens were challenging almost every vestige of legal segregation existing in the nation, especially in the South. Segregation in schools, housing and transportation rested upon the doctrine of "separate but equal" facilities established before the turn of the century in the case of *Plessy* v. *Ferguson*. The NAACP began its fight in the lower federal courts with the expressed purpose of undermining and ultimately changing the *Plessy* doctrine. In some cases, segregation was struck down on grounds that the separate facilities maintained for blacks were not in fact equal. The *Plessy* doctrine was not abandoned until 1954 in the historic case of *Brown* v. *Board of Education,* but the pattern of the decision of the federal courts was changing and it was obvious that the *Plessy* doctrine was being undermined.

Between 1948 and 1954, Judge Parker wrote seven opinions involving the constitutionality of racial segregation. In December, 1948 he handed down an opinion in the case of *County School Board of Chesterfield County* v. *Freeman* sustaining a district court decision holding unequal salaries for black teachers unconstitutional. As authority, Parker cited his own decision in *Alston* v. *School Board of City of Norfolk* which the Supreme Court had approved by refusing to review. The following year in the case of *Baskin* v.

Brown he again struck down efforts of the Democratic party in South Carolina to prevent Blacks from voting in primary elections. After Parker's decision in *Rice* v. *Elmore*, two years previously, the defendants formed private clubs, vested control of the primaries in their hands, and barred Blacks from gaining membership in the clubs. Judge Parker in a strongly worded opinion held such maneuvers to be unconstitutional, citing as authority his decision in *Rice* v. *Elmore*, and the series of Supreme Court decisions that supported that ruling.

In July, 1950 in the case of *Boyer* v. *Garrett*, Parker held that racial segregation in the public parks and playgrounds of the city of Baltimore was not unconstitutional under the policy of the Supreme Court as expressed in the *Plessy* case. Though appellants argued strongly that the authority of that case was so weak that the Court should not consider itself bound, Parker sustained the lower court decision which was based squarely on it. In answer to the attack on the authority of the *Plessy* case, he responded:

> We do not think, however, that we are at liberty thus to disregard a decision of the Supreme Court which that court has not seen fit to overrule and which it expressly refrained from re-examining, although urged to do so, in the very recent case of *Sweatt* v. *Painter* (70 S. Ct. 848). It is for the Supreme Court, not us, to overrule its decisions or to hold them outmoded.

Prelude To *Brown* v. *Board of Education*

The most significant decision rendered by Judge Parker prior to 1954 involving racial segregation was in the case of *Briggs* v. *Elliot,* decided in June, 1951. A black man, Harry

Briggs, Jr., in the interest of himself and others similarly situated, brought suit against school authorities in Clarendon County, South Carolina, seeking a declaratory judgement and injunctive relief of the effect that black schools in District 22 were not equal to white schools and were therefore in violation of the equal protection clause of the Fourteenth Amendment. He further charged that those provisions of the Constitution of the state of South Carolina requiring segregation of the races in the public schools were, in themselves, a denial of equal protection of the laws. In effect, Briggs asked the Court to rule that segregated schools *per se* were unconstitutional.

District Judge J. Waties Waring of Charleston notified Judge Parker that since a question of constitutionality was involved, a three-judge court would have to be convened to hear the case. Since Parker customarily sat on all such three-judge courts in North and South Carolina he appointed himself, along with District Judge George Bell Timmerman of Columbia, S. C., to join Waring in the case.

In the hearing the state authorities readily admitted that black schools in Clarendon County were not equal to the schools provided for white people. They argued, however, that these conditions resulted from limited financial resources rather than a deliberate policy of discrimination against black schools. Furthermore, the defendants pointed out that the state legislature had made provisions for a giant bond issue to finance the equalization of black schools and that this task would be accomplished within the immediate future. In the light of this admission by the state of South Carolina the only issue in dispute was the constitutionality of segregated schools *per se*.

The plaintiffs called a large number of witnesses, including professional educators and sociologists, who testified to the adverse effects of segregation on the learning opportunities of black children. The purpose of such testimony was to demonstrate that unequal learning opportunities amounted to a denial of equal protection of the laws. The defendants called very few witnesses. Evidently they were relying on existing precedents of the Supreme Court to give them a victory in the case.

In conference Parker and Timmerman agreed that the law governing both questions was well settled by previously established precedents of the Supreme Court. Judge Waring, however, was doubtful and indicated that he might dissent from the views of the majority. When Parker, who had elected to write the opinion for the court, sent his draft to Waring for criticism the Charleston judge responded saying that he definitely would file a dissent. Before the opinion was officially announced numerous judges and lawyers in other states asked Parker for copies. One of these requests is of particular interest. On June 25, two days after the opinion was handed down, Judge Walter A. Huxman of Topeka, Kansas, wrote that he was hearing that day a case of like nature and would like to have a copy of Parker's opinion and a statement as to the findings of fact. He added, "I know it will be helpful to us when we come to the consideration of the questions in this case." The case he was referring to was *Brown* v. *Board of Education*.

Concerning the first issue, Judge Parker, speaking for himself and Judge Timmerman, and therefore the Court, pointed out that where separate school systems are maintained the states must provide equal facilities and opportunities to both races. He cited a series of Supreme Court decisions that clearly established that unequal facilities were in direct conflict with the requirements of the Fourteenth Amendment. Plaintiffs were, therefore, clearly entitled to a declaratory judgement to the effect that their schools were unequal and to a mandatory injunction ordering the state of South Carolina to equalize its school systems without delay. He ruled, however, that in view of the above mentioned bond issue and the efforts of the state to equalize its schools, the proper function of the court was not to tell the state how to accomplish its task but merely to assure that it proceeded to equalize its school systems. He ordered South Carolina to take action and to report its progress within a period of six months.

On the second issue, the three judges were faced squarely with the question of the constitutionality of segregated schools *per se*. This was a test case designed specifically for that purpose and was destined to reach the Supreme Court regardless of the decision reached by the three-judge district court. With Thurgood Marshall of New York City and the Attorney General of South Carolina, each with a corps of supporting lawyers, representing the contesting parties, this most important issue was debated before the court "with a good deal of feeling on both sides."

In denying injunctive relief to the plaintiffs and upholding the constitutionality of segregated school systems Judge Parker relied for authority on several different considerations. At the outset he declared that so long as equality was maintained in the schools, the question as to whether or not children of different races would or would not be educated in the same schools was a matter which depended solely upon the legislative policies of the several states. In the absence of inequalities the federal courts were without power to interfere. Citing as authority Mr. Justice Harlan's opinion for a unanimous court in the case of *Cumming* v. *County Board of Education,* he said:

> One of the great virtues of our constitutional system is that, while the federal government protects the fundamental rights of the individual, it leaves to the several states the solution of local problems. In a country with a great expanse of territory with people of widely differing customs and ideas, local self-government in local matters is essential to the strength and unity of the country as a whole. It is universally held, therefore, that each stae shall determine for itself, subject to the observances of the fundamental rights and liberties guaranteed by the federal Constitution, how it shall exercise its police power, i. e., the power to legislate with respect to the safety, morals, and general welfare. And in no field is this right of the several states more clearly recognized than in that of public education.

Though Parker apparently believed firmly that such questions were best left to local authorities, he did not depend upon this reasoning alone to support his decision. The principle basis upon which he rested his decision was the long series of Supreme Court decisions, beginning with *Plessy* v. *Ferguson,* which established the doctrine that educating the children of different races in different school systems was not a violation of the Constitution so long as the facilities and opportunities remained equal. Quoting at length from the *Plessy* decision Parker added his own italics for emphasis to the following portion of that opinion.

> In determining the question of reasonableness, it [the state] is at liberty to act with reference to the usages, customs, and traditions of the people, and with a view to the protection of their comfort, and the preservation of the public peace and good order.

To further strengthen his reliance on Supreme Court precedents, Parker cited and discussed with emphasis the case of *Gong Lum* v. *Rice*. He declared that this case could not be distinguished because it was "directly in point and absolutely controlling upon us so long as it stands unreversed by the Supreme Court." In essence, this decision involved the refusal of the Supreme Court to strike down as unconstitutional a state's decision to exclude a child of Chinese parentage from a school reserved for white children. Parker then pointed out that seventeen states had statutes or constitutional provisions requiring segregated schools and that wherever such requirements had been challenged their constitutionality had been upheld without question. Relative to the existence of Supreme Court decisions which could be interpreted to contradict his reading of the law, he had this to say:

> No cases have been cited to us holding that such legislation is violative of the Fourteenth Amendment. We know of none, and diligent search of the authorities has failed to reveal any.

In answer to plaintiff's reliance upon such cases as *Sweatt* v. *Painter, McLaurin* v. *Oklahoma State Regents,* and *McKissick* v. *Carmichael,* Parker distinguished them by pointing out that they dealt with professional schools in states where similar facilities for blacks were either non-existent or clearly of inferior quality. He added that in *Sweatt* v. *Painter* the Supreme Court had refused to overrule the *Plessy* case although it had been strongly urged to do so. Parker then proceeded to draw a sharp distinction between segregated professional schools and segregated public schools, relative to the requirements of the Constitution.

Observing that few states could provide equal professional schools on a segregated basis because of the expense involved and the inability to insure equality of professional contacts, he said:

> The problem of segregation at the common school level is a very different one. At this level, as good as education can be afforded in Negro schools as in white schools and the thought of establishing professional contacts does not enter the picture. Moreover, education at this level is not a matter of voluntary choice on the part of the student but of compulsion by the state. The student is taken from the control of the family during school hours by compulsion of law and placed in control of the school, where he must associate with his fellow students. The law thus provided that the school shall supplement the work of the parent in the training of the child and in doing so it is entering a delicate field and one fraught with tensions and difficulties. In formulating educational policy at the common school level, therefore, the law must take account, not merely of the matter of affording instruction to the student, but also of the wishes of the parent as to the upbringing of the child and his associates in the formative period of childhood and adolescence. If public education is to have the support of the people through their legislatures, it must not go contrary to what they deem for the best interest of their children.

In the latter part of the opinion Parker drew upon his firmly held convictions concerning the proper function of the federal courts. It should be recalled here that Parker, throughout his long career in public life, held firm to the view that federalism was essential to the national health and the preservation of popular government in a large and diverse society. In answer to the arguments of the contesting parties relative to the effects of segregation or integration on the education of young children, Parker held that such questions did not involve constitutional rights but were matters of legislative policy. Decisions governing such matters should be made, "not in vacuo or with doctrinaire disregard of existing conditions, but in realistic approach to the situation to which it is applied." It followed then, he continued, that state legislatures should determine the wisdom and feasibility of a particular educational policy and should consider the relationships existing between the races and the tensions likely to result if efforts were made to educate the children of the two races in the same schools. He added:

> The federal courts would be going far outside their constitutional function were they to attempt to prescribe educational policies for the states in such matters, however desirable such policies might be in the opinion of some sociologists and educators. For the federal courts to do so would result, not only in interference with local affairs by an agency of the federal government but also in the substitution of the judicial for the legislative process in what is essentially a legislative matter.

Concluding, Parker indicated that in the final analysis his decision was based squarely on the requirements of the law as declared by the Supreme Court:

> We think that this conclusion is supported by overwhelming authority which we are not at liberty to disregard on the basis of theories advanced by a few educators and sociologists. Even if we felt at liberty to disregard other authorities, we may not ignore the unreversed decisions of the Supreme Court of the United States which are squarely in point and conclusive of the question before us.... It is for the Supreme Court, not us, to overrule its decisions or to hold them outmoded.

Judge Waring filed a lengthy and impassioned dissent against the opinion of the majority. His statement was, in the truest sense of the term, an appeal to the "brooding spirit of the law." Citing many of the same cases relied on by Parker, but viewing them in a different light and placing a different interpretation upon their relevance to the question of segregated schools, the Charleston judge literally thundered against the social system which maintained racial segregation and against the trend in judicial decisions which had perverted the true meaning and intent of the Fourteenth Amendment. In essence, Judge Waring declared that the majority had failed to come to grips with the constitutionality of legal segregation which was the principal issue in the case. Basing his dissent on what he felt the Constitution *should* require in the matter rather than on what the Supreme Court had actually said about it in previous cases, Waring ended his opinion with the declaration that "segregation is *per se* inequality."

Judge Waring refused to sign the court order directing South Carolina to equalize its school systems and soon thereafter retired from active service on the bench. The case went on to the Supreme Court but was remanded with instructions to reconsider in the light of changed circumstances growing out of South Carolina's efforts to equalize its schools. The rehearing was scheduled after Waring's retirement date but Parker designated him to sit because it was customary for the original court to rehear a case. And as a retired Judge, Waring was legally qualified to continue working if he chose to do so. Parker reconvened the court but Judge Waring refused the designation, saying, "I would not be willing to accept a designation to sit with you in the case or take any part in it." Circuit Judge Armistead Dobie of Charlottesville, Virginia was designated to sit and the three judges unanimously affirmed the earlier decision on the same legal grounds.

In these pre-1954 decisions, Judge Parker followed what he believed to be the law as declared by the Supreme Court. In the voting rights, teacher's salaries and transportation cases, he struck down racial discrimination because it was clear to him that such practices were in violation of the Constitution. In cases dealing with segregation in public schools, public parks and playgrounds, however, he refused to do so on grounds that controlling precedents in these areas had not been reversed by the Supreme Court.

Judge Parker's reasoning and adherence to precedent in the *Briggs* case stands out in bold relief when compared to his reasoning and disregard for precedent in the second flag salute case in 1942. In the flag salute case, he refused to be bound by a precedent of the Supreme Court, which was barely two years old, that he believed to be wrong. He dismissed it as a binding authority and decided the case in accordance with his own interpretation of the Constitution. He looked forward to what a new Supreme Court would likely do with the issue rather than backward at what an old Court had done with precisely the same set of facts. He delved behind decisions, which he viewed not as law but as expressions of law, and based his reasoning on what he personally believed the Constitution required in the area of religious freedom.

The *Briggs* decision was more technical in nature, ultimately relying on the letter of the *Plessy* rule as embodied in a precedent that was over fifty years old. Though unreversed, the rule was not in good standing in 1951 and was becoming less so with each passing year. Judge Parker was a perceptive jurist with an expert knowledge of the law. It is inconceivable that he was unaware of what the Supreme Court would ultimately do in the matter of segregated schools. Yet he did not engage in "nose counting," as he had done in the *Barnette* case in order to anticipate the Supreme Court, but chose instead to rely on what he referred to as the "well settled" principles of the law as preserved by the Supreme Court's own decisions. In contrast to his treatment of the flag salute precedent, he pointedly declared that it was the business of the Supreme Court to overrule its own decisions if it believed them to be erroneous. And, on one occasion in the opinion, he remarked that "the members of the judiciary have no more right to read their ideas of sociology into the Constitution than their ideas of economics."

In the *Briggs* case Parker was confronted with the most demanding and a far reaching issue to come before the federal Judiciary in the Twentieth Century. It seems not too much to suggest that Judge Parker knew in his own mind that his decision would not survive once the Supreme Court decided to reconsider the question. For many months prior to 1951 in letters to friends and associates on the bench he had expressed deep concern about the racial situation. He frequently voiced the belief that its solution depended upon due deliberation, cautious progress with adequate consideration given to the consequences of change, and dependence upon the Christian spirit as expressed through the orderly processes of law.

Parker was acutely aware of the possible consequences in the South of an abrupt change in the legal validity of segregation in the public schools. He obviously believed that the problem should best be solved by legislative action on a state by state basis, where local customs, as well as the requirements of the Constitution would receive consideration. In view of the unlikelihood of legislative action to this effect in the South, Parker certainly knew that the federal courts would have to take the lead. In the face of unreversed decisions of the Supreme Court, however, and in the belief that a decision of such magnitude should be made by the highest judicial tribunal in the land, Judge Parker upheld the constitutionality of segregation in the public schools and left it to justices of the Supreme Court to reverse him, and themselves, if the decision was wrong. His departure from precedent in the flag salute case was a minor matter, no great social upheaval would occur regardless of how the case was resolved, despite the importance of the principle involved. Racial segregation in the schools was another question entirely. If the federal judiciary was going to decide the issue, only a unanimous Supreme Court should reverse a precedent that had been in place for over a half-century and upon which the social system of a large section of the country was based. Lower federal court judges could not go their own ways, even for a short period of time, on such an explosive issue, especially given the certain difficulties in implementing the decision in the months and years that were to follow.

The decision was, of course, appealed and, along with three other cases of like nature from the appellate courts, was placed on the Supreme Court docket for the 1952 term. After considerable delay, and much maneuvering by Chief Justice Earl Warren, the Supreme Court handed down its long awaited opinion under the title of *Brown* v. *Board of Education of Topeka,* holding that segregation *per se* in the public schools was in violation of the Fourteenth Amendment to the Constitution. A year later the final decree was issued, remanding the four cases to the lower courts with instructions to require the defendants to begin a prompt and reasonable start toward compliance with the court's decision. A careful reading of Judge Parker's letters, speeches, memoranda and subsequent opinions does not reveal a single critical remark about the new interpretation of the Constitution. This is instructive because in letters to his colleagues on other matters over the years he was not reluctant to express disapproval of what the Supreme Court had done if he believed its decisions were incorrect.

Implementing The Brown Decision

In the four years between the Supreme Court's reversal of his decision in the *Briggs* case and his death in 1958, Judge Parker wrote seventeen opinions dealing with the implementation of the *Brown* decision. The pattern of Parker's decision-making in these cases is clear: He carried out his duty to implement the decisions of the Supreme Court. Three of these decisions are representative of what he believed to be required by the law of the *Brown* decision.

In July, 1955, Parker handed down his third opinion in the case of *Briggs* v. *Elliott*. The Supreme court remand had instructed the lower courts to enter such orders and decrees necessary to admit pupils to the public schools on a non-discriminatory basis. The first draft of the opinion contains a paragraph in which Judge Parker attempted to persuade those opposed to the new policy that survival of the constitutional system depended upon the lower federal courts, and the people generally, following the law as declared by the Supreme Court. After observing that the Constitution was an enduring instrument which had to be reinterpreted to meet the needs of each generation, he wrote:

> Court decisions are not the law but merely evidences of law; and it not infrequently happens that, as a result of changed conditions, decisions are overruled in what is thought to be a more correct application of constitutional principles to the existing conditions. When this occurs, the overruling decisions of the Supreme Court must be accepted as the correct statement of the law, otherwise our governmental system will not work and anarchy will result. They will be accepted by this court, and we think, by law abiding people generally.

For reasons which cannot be determined Judge Parker deleted this paragraph from his next draft. In the official opinion he began by pointing out that his court in its prior decision had followed what it conceived to be the law as previously laid down by the Supreme Court. He then included the sense of the deleted paragraph in this statement.

> Whatever may have been the view of this court as to the law when the case was originally before us, it is our duty now to accept the law as declared by the Supreme Court.

After that brief statement, but before quoting from the *Brown* decision in which the Supreme Court spoke for itself, Parker interjected a lengthy explanation as to what the *Brown* decision did not require of the states. As mentioned above he was much concerned about how the new policy would be received in the South and the effect of this reception of relations between the races. This attempt to explain in detail the exact meaning of the *Brown* decision was designed to soften its impact on the troubled region and to encourage hard core opponents of integrated schools to accept the law peaceably. Declaring that it was his duty to accept the law as determined by the Supreme Court, he added:

> Having said this, it is important that we point out exactly what the Supreme Court has decided and what it has not decided in this case. It has not decided that the federal courts are to take over or regulate the public schools of the states. It has not decided that the states must mix persons of different races in the schools or must require them to attend schools or must deprive them of the right of choosing the schools they attend. What it has decided, and all that it has decided, is that a state may not deny to any person on account of race the right to attend any school that it maintains. This, under the decision of the Supreme Court, the state may not do directly or indirectly; but if the schools which it maintains are open to children of all races, no violation of the Constitution is involved even though the children of different races voluntarily attend different schools, as they attend different churches. Nothing in the Constitution or in the decision of the Supreme Court takes away from the people freedom to choose the schools they attend. The Constitution, in other words, does not require integration. It merely forbids discrimination. It does not forbid such segregation as occurs as the result of voluntary action. It merely forbids the use of governmental power to enforce segregation. The Fourteenth Amendment is a limitation upon the exercise of power by the state or state agencies, not a limitation upon the freedom of individuals.

Judge Parker's reaction to the so-called pupil placement laws passed by some states reveals something of his attitude toward the courts' responsibilities in implementing the *Brown* decision. Blacks in Old Fort, North Carolina, had brought suit in the federal court seeking equal education facilities in that town. The case was pending when the *Brown* case was decided. Acting upon that decision the district judge dismissed the case as moot because the relief sought [separate but equal facilities] was no longer appropriate under the new policy of the Supreme Court. Hearing the case, *Carson* v. *Board of Education of McDowell County,* on appeal Parker reversed the lower court and ordered the judge to reconsider the matter in the light of the North Carolina Pupil Placement Law which had just been passed.

When the district judge stayed the proceedings to allow supplemental pleadings, the plaintiffs petitioned the Fourth Circuit Court of Appeals for a writ of mandamus compelling the district judge to vacate his stay order and to grant the relief requested. In *Carson* v. *Warlick,* handed down in November, 1956, Parker refused to grant the mandamus on grounds that the plaintiffs had not availed themselves of the administrative remedies provided by the state in its Pupil Placement Law. He declared that judicial remedies, though available, could not be granted by the federal courts until these administrative remedies had been exhausted.

In a series of cases, the most important of which was *School Board of the City of Charlottesville* v. *Allen,* Judge Parker ordered school boards in the state of Virginia to take immediate steps toward admitting children to the public schools without regard to race. In Parker's mind the Pupil Placement Law passed by the Virginia legislature offered no adequate remedy to blacks because it clearly reflected the state's determination to preserve racial segregation in the school systems. In providing for the closing schools, and the withdrawal of funds from integrated schools, the law was an obstruction of the law as declared by the Supreme Court rather than an instrument of implementation.

The Virginia authorities were guilty of undue delay and their dilatory tactics clearly manifested an attitude of intransigence. The Pupil Placement Law was nothing more than a device to obstruct the law and, because of its purpose as well as its effect, was contrary to the Constitution. Injunctions, therefore, had to be issued to dispel the misapprehension of schools authorities as to their obligations under the law and to insure compliance with constitutional requirements as interpreted by the Supreme Court.

Parker, however, believed that the Pupil Placement Law passed by the North Carolina General Assembly met the test of constitutionality. He felt that it provided equitable administrative procedures whereby individual students regardless of race could seek reassignment to different schools. The federal courts, therefore, should not enter the picture so long as the law was administered fairly.

Judge Parker had no sympathy with the view that federal judges should involve themselves in the operation of the public schools or in the procedures designed for the enrollment of individual pupils in the schools. In the *Carson* case cited above, he said:

> Somebody must enroll the pupils in the school. They cannot enroll themselves; and we think of no one better qualified to undertake the task than the officials of the schools and the school boards having the schools in charge. It is to be presumed that these will obey the law, observe the standards prescribed by the legislature, and avoid the discrimination on the account of race which the Constitution forbids. Not until they have been applied to and have failed to give relief should the courts be asked to interfere in school administration.

In the Virginia cases the legislative remedies were inadequate. Thus Parker, without hesitation, ordered the school boards to integrate the schools. In North Carolina, where the legislative remedies were considered to be adequate and equitable, Parker held that they must be exhausted before any application for relief from the federal courts would be considered. Judge Parker died in 1958 after suffering a heart attack in the lobby of the Mayflower Hotel in Washington, D. C. Thus he did not live to see how the controversy over the meaning of the Supreme Court's ruling in the *Brown* case would develop or how subsequent court decisions would continue to refine the meaning of the Constitution on the question of racial discrimination. He may or may not have agreed with some of these decisions, but he would have certainly agreed that the great principles of the Constitution could only be preserved if they were modernized to meet the needs of living generation. And, he would have remained firm in his conviction that it was the duty of the federal courts, not pressure groups, political majorities or concentrations of political and economic power, to change the meaning of the fundamental law.

Some critics of Judge Parker have charged that his repeated explanations of the exact meaning of the *Brown* case contributed to the delay in carrying out the Supreme Court's directive to move forward with "all deliberate speed" in integrating public schools. His colleague on the Fourth Circuit Court, Judge Simon Sobeloff, once wrote, "I know how earnestly you have endeavored to moderate emotions in this area of race relations, and you have taken occasion to say in our court's opinions that which would help to lessen resistance to the Supreme Court's decision." Sobeloff then informed Parker that certain members of the press and some public leaders, on both sides of the question, were using his remarks to argue that nothing really needed to be changed.

Judge Parker was fully aware of this. But he felt that his interpretation of the *Brown* case was the correct interpretation and that peaceful and harmonious change in the area of race relations depended upon widespread under-standing of exactly what the law required and what it did not. Liberty in America was liberty under the law; he was not seeking to frustrate the law, but to encourage its peaceful acceptance. His duty as a judge allowed him no other course.

VIII

A Liberal
In
The American Pattern

The true liberal is ever mindful of preserving, amid the changing forms of life, those values which are eternal.

John J. Parker

Judge Parker did not like labels. He distrusted those who wore them, and he was suspicious of any effort to reshape society and politics according to dogma or some single view of the future. Professor Horace Williams was correct when he wrote to Parker in 1930: "Nobody will succeed in putting a label on you." And Judge Morris Soper's remark twenty-eight years later, as close to the mark as it was, that Judge Parker was "a staunch and fundamental constitutionalist," shadows somewhat the flexibility that was such an important element in his public philosophy. Perhaps the term, "A Liberal in the American Pattern," comes closest to describing Judge Parker's long career as a public servant. Indeed, this description is one he used himself in paying honor to Chief Justice Harlan Fiske Stone, a great jurist whose views were remarkably similar to his own.

Despite his sternness, adherence to principle, self-confidence and certainty of his own beliefs, there was nothing of the doctrinaire in John J. Parker. He was an eminently pragmatic man in his views on politics and the Constitution. The great truths and principles of the Constitution that he talked so much about were not words written in stone. They were broad-guaged and open-ended rules for public life that had evolved from experience. It was the duty of public leaders, especially judges, to reinterpret these principles and apply them to public life in the light of changing needs, conditions and modes of thought.

At the heart of Parker's public philosophy was a belief in the liberty of individuals, their right to remain free to develop themselves and accept responsibility for their own actions and welfare. The proper function of government was to protect these rights against forces and conditions over which people had no control: external enemies, domestic violence, social or cultural stagnation that prevented reform of the law, economic emergencies, concentrations of financial power, and most important, the powers of the state itself. Rigid adherence to outdated interpretations of the Constitution could not provide this protection; only a flexible approach to the meaning of eternal values could do this, an approach that recognized court decisions as expressions of the law, not the law itself.

In the American context, Judge Parker believed that experience had proven the value and usefulness of the concepts of federalism, separation of powers and the Bill of Rights as interpreted by an independent judiciary. But these were not fixed concepts, they were flexible constitutional practices evolving through time in response to experience and common sense. Adherence to them did not dictate the future; it allowed free men to shape their own futures, to maintain that tenuous balance between liberty and restraint that made constitutional democracy an acceptable form of public order. Judge Parker believed self-government to be the only form of public order fit for men, and he believed the American experience should and could serve as a model for free men everywhere. But he knew that American democracy was still an experiment, an experiment that had worked reasonably well because of the spirit of the people and the guiding hand of the Constitution. The future of democracy, however, was never secure because of the tendency of men to lose sight of fundamental principles and to succumb to narrow interests, greed or some passionate fixation on a single goal. Although he had great faith in the people when they were wisely led, he remained mindful, and sometimes fearful, about the future.

As a young politician seeking the governorship of North Carolina in 1920, he saw stagnation and the refusal of the political parties to reform themselves as a danger to democracy. As a federal judge during the Great Depression, he was fearful that rigid interpretations of the Constitution would prevent the expansion of the regulatory powers of the federal government and thereby prevent the use of public authority to protect the people from economic catastrophe. Then when expanded governmental powers were held constitutional, he called for even greater vigilance in the protection of liberty against the power of the state. During the Cold War, he rejected the "mawkish sentimentality" underlying the arguments of those who believed that the Constitution granted no power to the government to protect itself from its own citizens who set out to change the system through conspiracy, deception and violence. And during his last years on the bench, he cautioned against an overly loose interpretation of the law which would allow the government to pursue a social policy, however well intended, that might prove to be disruptive of public order.

Judge Parker believed in the organic view of society and politics. Government rested upon community, but community could not be created by administration; it had to be created by the people themselves living and working through non-governmental institutions. Throughout his long career, but especially near the end, Parker feared the loss of historical perspective, discipline, patience, good will and common sense. Democracy could not defend itself; only men and women of good judgement, determination, a sense of fair play and an appreciation for the history of their own institutions could do this. He was an optimist, not a calamity-howler. He lectured about the virtues of America rather than its vices and he attempted to inspire the people, not condemn them. But underlying his optimism about the future was a nagging fear that American democracy under stress could fall prey to passion in its politics and to a corruption of its language that erased the distinction between what was public and what should remain private. But most of all he feared a retreat into ideology where political majorities would attempt to shape the future according to some closed system of truth. In Judge Parker's public philosophy, free men could only remain free if their future remained open, to be shaped by themselves according to the needs, conditions and circumstances of their own times. His hope was that future generations would cling to those eternal values embodied in the American Constitution that had shaped and preserved a system of liberty under the law.

Appendix

Property Rights Cases 1925-1937

Kelleher v. French, 22 F (2d) 341 (1927).

Lynchburg Traction and Light Co. v. City of Lynchburg, 16 F (2d) 763 (1927).

Doscher v. Query, 21 F (2d) 521 (1927).

United States v. Lindgren, 28 F (2d) 725 (1928).

Ferris v. Wilbur, 27 F (2d) 262 (1928).

Suncrest Lumber Co. v. N. C. Park Commission, 30 F (2d) 121 (1929).

Carolina and N. W. Ry. Co. v. Town of Lincolnton, 33 F (2d) 719 (1929).

United States v. Tyler, 33 F (2d) 724 (1929).

Wheeling Corrugating Co. v. McManigal. 41 F (2d) 593 (1930).

Standard Oil Co. of New Jersey v. City of Charlottesville, 42 F (2d) 88 (1930).

Carolina and N. W. Ry. Co. v. Town of Clover, 46 F (2d) 395 (1931).

South Carolina Power Co. v. South Carolina Tax Commission, 52 F (2d) 515 (1931).

United States v. Wright, 53 F (2d) 301 (1931).

Southern Grocery Stores v. South Carolina Tax Commission, 55 F (2d) (1931-1932).

Mayor and City Council of Baltimore v. Williams, 61 F (2d) 374 (1932).

Link v. Receivers of Seaboard Air Line Ry. Co., 73 F (2d) 149 (1934).

Campbell v. Alleghany Corp., 75 F (2d) 947 (1935).

Eley v. Gamble, 75 F (2d) 171 (1935).

Bradford v. Fahey, 76 F (2d) 628 (1935).

Duke Power Co. v. South Carolina Tax Commission, 81 F (2d) 513 (1936).

Greenwood Couty v. Duke Power Co., 81 F (2d) 986 (1936).

Virginia Ry. Co. v. System Federation No. 40, 84 F (2d) 641 (1936).

Wright v. Vinton Bank, 85 F (2d) 973 (1936).

White Packing Co. v. Robertson, 89 F (2d) 775 (1937).

Duke Power Co. v. Greenwood County, 91 F (2d) 665 (1937).

Civil Liberty Cases 1925-1958

Henderson v. United States, 12 F (2d) 528 (1926).

Neal v. United States, 22 F (2d) 52 (1927).

Dodson v. United States, 23 F (2d) 401 (1928).

Lisansky v. United States, 31 F (2d) 346 (1929).

City of Richmond v. Deans, 37 F (2d) 712 (1930).

Wallace v. Currin, 95 F (2d) 856 (1938).

Isgrig v. United States, 109 F (2d) 131 (1940).

Alston v. School Board of City of Norfolk, 112 F (2d) 992 (1940).

Smith v. Blackwell, 115 F (2d) 186 (1940).

Bersio v. United States, 124 F (2d) 310 (1941).

Mitchell v. Yovell, 130 F (2d) 880 (1942).

Barnette v. West Virginia State Board of Education, 47 F Supp. 251 (1942).

Sanderlin v. Smyth, 138 F (2d) 729 (1943).

Z. L. Kanich v. United States, 139 F (2d) 1016 (1944).

Barber v. United States, 142 F (2d) 805 (1944).

Purcell v. Somers, 145 F (2d) 979 (1944).

Schwab v. Coleman, 145 F (2d) 672 (1944).

Bowels v. American Brewery, 146 F (2d) 842 (1945).

Michael v. Cockerell, 161 F (2d) 163 (1947).

Rice v. Elmore, 165 F (2d) 387 (1947).

Frankfeld v. United States, 198 F (2d) (1952).

Scales v. United States, 227 F (2d) 581 (1955).

Briggs v. Elliott, 98 F. Supp. 529 (1951).

Briggs v. Elliott, 103 F. Supp. 920 (1951).

Baskin v. Brown, 174 F (2d) 391 (1949).

Boyer v. Garrett, 183 F (2d) 582 (1950).

Butler v. Thompson, 184 F (2d) 526 (1950).

Carolina Coach Co. v. Williams, F (2d) 408 (1953).

County School Board of Chesterfield County v. Freeman, 171.

Briggs v. Elliott, 132 F. Supp. 776 (1955).

Davis v. School Board of Prince Edward County, 142 F. Supp. 616 (1956).

Carson v. Board of Education of McDowell County, 227 F (2d) 789 (1955).

Carson v. Warlick, 238 F (2d) 724 (1956).

Allen v. County School Board of Prince Edward County, 249 F (2d) 462 (1957).

School Board of the City of Charlottesville v. Allen, 240 F (2d) 59 (1956).

Dawson v. Mayor and City Council of Baltimore City, 220 F (2d) 386 (1955).

Fleming v. S. C. Electric and Gas Company, 224 F (2d) 752 (1955).

Department of Conservation and Development v. Tate, 231 F (2d) 615 (1956).

Hood v. Board of Trustees of Sumter County, 232 F (2d) 626 (1956).

Clark v. Flory, 237 F (2d) 587 (1956).

City of Greensboro v. Simpkins, 246 F (2d) 425 (1957).

County School Board of Arligton County v. Thompson, 252 F (2d) 929 (1958).

Slade v. Board of Education of Harford County, 252 F (2d) 291 (1958).

Bryan v. Austin, 148 F. Supp. 563 (1957).

School Board of City of Newport News v. Atkins, 246 F (2d) 325 (1957).

Lassiter v. Taylor, 152 F. Supp. 295 (1957).

Articles by John J. Parker

"Erie v. Tomkins in Retrospect: An Analysis of Its Area and Limits," *American Bar Association Journal,* XXXV (January, 1949), 19-22, 83-86.

"The Federal Jurisdiction and Recent Attacks Upon It," *American Bar Association Journal,* XVIII (July, 1932), 433-439, 479.

"The Crisis in Constitutional Government," *Commercial Law Journal* , (August, 1934), 378-383.

"Enforcement of Professional Ethics," *American Bar Association Journal* XXI (August, 1935), 514-518.

"The Lawyer in A Democracy," *Speeches and Articles,* Parker Collection, Wilson Library, University of North Carolina at Chapel Hill.

"Is the Constitution Passing?" *Speeches and Articles,* Parker Collection, Wilson Library, University of North Carolina at Chapel Hill.

"Schools of Jurisprudence in the Federal System," *Journal of the American Judicature Society,* XXIII (June, 1939), 5-10.

Opening Address of the Legal Institute on Modern Federal Administrative Law, April 28, 1939, Richmond, Virginia. *Annual Reports, Virginia State Bar Association,* LI, 1939.

"Democracy and Constitutional Government," *American Bar Association Journal*, XXVI (January, 1940), 52-56.

"Improving the Administration of Justice," *American Bar Association Journal*, XXVI I (February, 1941), 71-76.

"The Work of the Committee," *American Bar Association Journal*, XXVII (December, 1941), 746-749.

"Leadership of the Bar in This Hour of Crisis," *American Bar Association Journal*. XXIX (January, 1943), 21-24.

"Honoring the Members of the Bar in the Armed Forces of the United States," *Speeches and Articles*, Parker Collection, Wilson Library, University of North Carolina at Chapel Hill.

"World Organization," *American Bar Association Journal*, XXIX (November, 1943), 617-622.

"The Integration of the Federal Judiciary," *Harvard Law Review*, LVI (January, 1943), 563-575.

"A Time for Greatness," *Michigan State Bar Journal*, XXIII (November, 1944), 498-511.

"World Government by Law," *Journal of the State Bar of California*, XX (May-June, 1945), 129-141.

"The Judicial Office in the United States," *New York University Law Review*, XXIII (April, 1948), 226-238.

"The Nuremberg Trial," printed by the Lawyer's Publishing Co. *Speeches and Articles*, Parker Collection, Wilson Library, University of North Carolina at Chapel Hill.

"Improving Appellate Methods," *New York University Law Review*, XXV (January, 1950), 1-15.

"The Federal Judicial System," *Federal Rules Decisions*, XIV (September, 1953), 361-370.

"A Profession, Not a Skilled Trade," *South Carolina Law Quarterly*, VIII (Winter, 1955), 179-188.

"The International Trial at Nuremberg on Giving Vitality to International Law," *The John Randolph Tucker Lectures*, published by the School of Law, Washington and Lee University, Lexington, Virginia, 1952.

"Improving the Administration of Justice," Proceedings of the Institute of Procedure, *Bulletin of the University of Georgia*, 1953, 7-14.

"Harlan Fiske Stone: A Liberal in the American Pattern," *Syracuse Law Review*, I (Spring, 1949), 1-8.

"The American Constitution and World Order Based on Law," *The Record of the Bar of the City of New York*, VIII (June, 1953), 267-285.

"The American Constitution and the Treaty Making Powers," *Washington University Law Quarterly*, Vol. 1954 (April, 1954), 115-131.

"Chief Justice Fred M. Vinson: Meeting the Challenge to Law and Order," *American Bar Association Journal,* XLI (April, 1955), 324-326, 363.

"Dual Sovereignty and the Federal Courts," *Northwestern University Law Review,* LI (September-October, 1956), 407-423.

"We Must Lead the World to Freedom and Justice," *American Bar Association Journal,* XLIV (January, 1958), 17-21.

"Race Relationships," *Church School Herald Journal* (December, 1944). Manuscript in Parker Papers, P. S. , Box 11, Folder 214.

Unpublished Materials

Burris, William C. "The Senate Rejects a Judge: A Study of the John J. Parker Case," Political Studies Program, Research Report No. 3, University of North Carolina. Chapel Hill: Department of Political Science, 1962.

Burris, William C. *John J. Parker and Supreme Court Policy: A Case Study in Judicial Control.* Unpublished Ph. D. Dissertation, Department of Political Science, The University of North Carolina at Chapel Hill, 1964.

The John J. Parker Papers. Southern Historical Collection, Wilson Library, The University of North Carolina at Chapel Hill.